ADVANCE PRAISE

"As a private wealth advisor for thirty-seven years, I can attest to the common sense and practical ideas in Chris Poch's new book, Money and Meaning: What I've Learned from Advising the Very Wealthy.

"But why do you really need to read this book? To take conventional ideas and use them as springboards for a financial life that reflects you. To grow your understanding of issues you don't often see discussed: the role of risk in any portfolio; the temptation to make portfolio choices from avoidance rather than long-term thinking; the role of money as a tool for your family.

"And hey, advisors! Get a ringside seat on what the smartest clients expect and how they are evaluating YOU!"

—MARY DEATHERAGE, CO-FOUNDER AND PRESIDENT OF
XCELERATE GROWTH PARTNERS, LLC, FORMER MANAGING
DIRECTOR AT MORGAN STANLEY PRIVATE WEALTH
ADVISORS, BARRON'S HALL OF FAME ADVISOR

"Friendships are forged out of shared experiences, celebrating successes and navigating crises. For many years, Chris has been my friend, as well as a partner, colleague, mentor, sounding board, and great supporter. Neither miles nor years have diminished our ability to have a conversation or gain an understanding of new areas of thought from each other.

"Throughout his successful career, Chris has always had his family, friends, and clients at the forefront of his thoughts and actions. Trust has to be earned, and Chris has earned my unwavering trust through all of his endeavors. His ability to listen is one of his most valuable traits. Chris is able to listen and then understands the needs of his clients in a remarkable way. As you will see, his writing aptitude brings to each a way of 'seeing' what is and what can be."

—SANDEE SMITH, RETIRED SENIOR VICE PRESIDENT AND FINANCIAL ADVISOR AT MORGAN STANLEY, NAMESAKE OF THE APIC SANDEE SMITH LEADERSHIP AWARD

"If you're an athlete, you're familiar with the idea of being 'in the zone.' Musicians call it being 'in the pocket.' It's that condition where you've been doing something so well for so long that success is not only expected but almost assured. That's where Chris Poch is as a financial advisor. There's not a market condition he hasn't seen, there's not a family dynamic he hasn't navigated, and there's not a significant portfolio risk or opportunity he hasn't considered. Chris has advised our family office for more than twenty years, and at this unprecedented moment of political and technological volatility, we are relying on his counsel more than ever."

—JOSEPH TRANFO, FOUNDER AND MANAGING PRINCIPAL OF BENEDICT CAPITAL, LLC

"I've known Chris Poch for forty years and trust his financial judgement and integrity so much I made him the Executor of my estate. Looking back over the years, I'm struck by how often he's been correct about the direction of markets. I didn't always listen to him, but if I had, I'm sure I'd have more money now."

—JOHN F. GROOM, FOUNDER OF GROOM VENTURES, LLC

"I've known Chris Poch for over thirty years, and from the very beginning, his honesty, confidence, intelligence, and client-first approach stood out. When a close friend needed trusted financial guidance, Chris was the first person I recommended—out of more than a hundred advisors. I have just as much confidence in him today as I did back then."

—H. WAYNE HUTTON, RETIRED REGIONAL DIRECTOR OF MORGAN STANLEY

"Chris has spent a lifetime collecting wisdom on one of life's most confounding questions: what is 'enough,' and how can we get it? I am grateful for the practical wisdom he shares with the world."

—JOHN CANDETO, FOUNDER AND MANAGING PARTNER OF PHRONESIS FUND, HOST OF *THE ART OF QUALITY IN INVESTING* PODCAST

"Chris Poch's Money and Meaning has synthesized his forty years of advising the very wealthy into a concise playbook on how the reader can leverage his deep market insights, expertise, and experience on effectively managing one's hard-earned wealth for future generations. His practical financial strategy sets out to impact your current approach to financial peace of mind and happiness for your family as it has for his own over three generations."

—MIKE RYAN, MANAGING PARTNER AT MGR CAPITAL, ADVISOR TO FOURTEEN UNICORN CEOS

"Chris Poch is the very definition of integrity, emotional intelligence, and thoughtfulness. During the more than twenty years that I've known Chris as an advisor, client, and friend, he has consistently displayed a remarkable ability to see people as they are and as they hope to be. He is someone I trust without reservation."

—DAVID J. RYNECKI, FOUNDER AND CEO OF BLUE HERON RESEARCH PARTNERS, AWARD-WINNING FINANCIAL JOURNALIST

"I met Chris about fifteen years ago at an investment luncheon where I was his guest. Over the years, our personal relationship has evolved from casual investment acquaintance to respected advisor to client to best friend as he transitioned from wirehouse, bulge-bracket brokerages to his own firm. He has invested the *time and made the extra effort to meet and get to know my wife and our children. He approaches his financial advisor role with a realistic long-term capital preservation and growth perspective that is focused on profitable, growing capital-light and dividend-paying companies. He communicates with us regularly and is a great listener and a curious questioner. He is open to new ideas and is constantly striving to improve his investment and relationship knowledge. His follow up to conversations and requests is perfect. As a result of his professionalism and personal style, we have recently named him as the successor trustee for our family trust.*

"Our family has complete trust and confidence that Chris will always give his best advice and act in our best interest. We are thankful that he accepted us as a client and feel blessed to have a professional and personal relationship with Chris."

—JOSEPH PISULA, PRIVATE CLIENT

"Nearly ten years ago, a thoughtful introduction from a close friend brought Chris into our lives. Recognizing the significant growth of our net worth, we realized the urgent need for an experienced wealth manager specializing in long-term investment strategies and retirement planning to provide us with comprehensive guidance and structure for our financial future.

"Since then, Chris, who has spent decades successfully managing wealth for high-net-worth families, has been a steadfast anchor for our family. His calm demeanor and clear, insightful communication have been particularly reassuring during turbulent market conditions. He often emphasizes that a long-term investment strategy, focused on companies with strong balance sheets and consistent dividends, is fundamental to wealth creation.

Additionally, he has been proactive in addressing our evolving estate planning needs, ensuring our family's future is secure. Chris has truly become a trusted advisor and an integral part of our lives. His reliable and unwavering guidance has had a transformative impact on us."

—AL TARASIUK, PRIVATE CLIENT

"Over the near-decade that we have worked with Chris Poch, we've shared the highs, a few lows, and wild swings that come during volatile markets and political transitions. Fortunately, Chris's steady hand and calming voice helped our psyches—and portfolio—remain fixed on our long-term objectives. As seniors, we came to understand that the preservation of wealth was far more important than the swings of the market. In years past, we watched our portfolio grow steadily. But in these trying times, protecting what we've built together has become the primary objective for us and our family."

—WILLIAM AND RENAY REGARDIE, PRIVATE CLIENT

"My wife and I are fortunate to have been working with Chris for nearly a decade. During that period, we have experienced financial market volatility as well as changes in personal and family circumstances. Chris has been a trusted resource and dependable sounding board throughout that time. His deep knowledge and experience as a wealth advisor and his thoughtful insights and guidance have been comforting when a level head was required. Having consulted with many investors and families during his career enables him to tailor those learnings to the specific issue at hand and to draw upon resources and contacts he has forged over forty-plus years to help resolve an issue.

"Chris has also taken a personal interest in getting to know our family and each of our children's situations. His advice and guidance have enabled our children to work with an experienced professional early in their lives and careers, putting them on their own paths toward building wealth and understanding financial markets.

"Trust, confidence, as well as successful and consistent financial performance sum up why we have peace of mind and appreciate working with Chris."

—Frank Golden, private client

"For more than ten years, my wife and I have looked to Chris as our family's most trusted financial advisor. This has been a volatile time in the market, and yet Chris, by his steady hand, reassuring tone, and tremendously insightful knowledge, has been the 'Rock of Gibraltar' in our financial lives.

"Chris has always taken the time to truly listen and understand what is important to us—not just financially but personally as well. As with any family, we have experienced changes and varying financial demands, and yet calling on his own long and trusted financial management skills, Chris has always provided the correct advice and the proper direction, all done in a caring, calm, and gentle manner.

"As an advisor, Chris strikes a unique balance of someone who is both steady and strategic, helping us feel secure in a constantly changing world. What truly stands out, however, is Chris's kindness, clarity, and the trust he has earned. What a great joy and a comfort it has been to have Chris as a guiding hand in our financial lives."

—Richard Milone, MD, private client

MONEY AND MEANING

MONEY

·AND·

MEANING

WHAT I'VE LEARNED FROM
ADVISING THE VERY WEALTHY

CHRISTOPHER F. POCH

Pm
61
Promethlum Publishing

MONEY AND MEANING
What I've Learned from Advising the Very Wealthy

FIRST EDITION

ISBN   978-1-5445-4916-3 *Hardcover*
        978-1-5445-4915-6 *Paperback*
        978-1-5445-4914-9 *Ebook*

Illustrations by Humna Qais.

CONTENTS

Free Financial Resources Developed by the Author............................*XVII*

Foreword ....*XXI*

Preface..*XXV*

PART I: MANAGING WEALTH

1. *Budget, Save, and Invest*..*5*

2. *How to Manage Your Family's Fortune*...*11*

3. *In Search of a Wealth Advisor* *27*

4. *How to Assemble a Team of Advisors*..*41*

5. *Get Great Service from Your Wealth Advisor*...............................*49*

6. *How to Be a Good Client*...*57*

7. *Putting Your Things in Order*..*65*

8. *How to Divide Without Conquering: Guidelines to an Executor*.....*71*

9. *It Takes More than Trust to Be a Good Trustee*............................*87*

PART II: MANAGING MONEY

10. *If Managing Money Is So Easy, Why Aren't More People Rich?*........*99*

11. *Develop Your Investment Philosophy*...*111*

12. *Investing for Future Cash Flow*..*121*

13. *You Just Came into a Pile of Money, Now What?* 133

14. *How Young People May Achieve Financial Independence* 141

15. *Secret to Staying Rich: Just Say No* 151

16. *Portfolio Management* 157

PART III: MANAGING TRANSITIONS

17. *Sacred Art of Listening* 171

18. *Successful Wealth Transitions: Involve—Inform—Entrust* 177

19. *How to Have the Prenuptial Conversation* 185

20. *When It's Time to Turn Over the Keys* 193

Concluding Thoughts 201

Acknowledgments 203

About the Author 207

Stay Connected 211

Disclaimer 213

FREE FINANCIAL RESOURCES DEVELOPED BY THE AUTHOR

WELCOME, READER!

To support you beyond these pages, I want to share resources designed to help you take actionable steps on your journey toward *peace of mind.*

Simply scan the QR code or click the link to access completely free tools developed for my own clients.

GOALS AND ASPIRATIONS TOOLKIT

A simple toolkit to help you identify your personal goals and aspirations and ensure you are on track to achieve the most important thing—peace of mind.

Scan: QR Code

INVESTMENT POLICY TOOLKIT
AND SAMPLE STATEMENT

Clarify your investment goals, risk tolerance, and attitude with this one-page worksheet and sample investment policy. This can serve as your personal blueprint for successful investing.

Scan: QR Code

Promethium Playbook: Investment Insights

Review years of investment insights to learn how Promethium Advisors anticipated market developments to protect and position portfolios to take advantage of changing market conditions.

Scan: QR Code

FOREWORD

"You have to leave; otherwise, they won't leave."

This is what the author of this book told me on 9/11 in a building just six blocks north of the World Trade Center. If everyone on the seventeenth floor saw me leave, he advised, they would feel it was ok for them to leave as well. I took his advice. I left. The building was evacuated, and our partners, colleagues, and friends arrived home safely.

What does this have to do with a book on wealth management? Everything. The author was cool, calm, and thinking of others on 9/11. This same man is cool and calm in today's volatile investment environment, thinking of you. Follow his advice, and you will arrive safely.

Chris Poch has had experiences and responsibilities unlike any other person on Wall Street. He had a very successful practice advising clients. Later, he created a second-to-none high-net-worth concierge service for Citigroup Smith Barney's largest clients. He traveled as part of a road show alongside Smith Barney's chairman, president, and senior management, educating the assembled clients and financial advisors on the outlook for financial assets and the markets. When you study this book, you will see how he learned from the highest-ranking executives and put his knowledge on the pages that follow.

This book is unique, in my opinion, in that the author

1. Explains an investor's choices regarding family planning issues,
2. Identifies potential solutions, and,
3. Most importantly, highlights what current fads to avoid.

These details are what make this book different.

I was at Smith Barney for thirty-two years and was proud to partner with Chris Poch and be part of a group of men and women who believed in running a business according to the following:

1. Do what's right for the client
2. Treat everyone with respect
3. Deliver outstanding results

The author of this book executes these mandates extraordinarily well. I think Chris's advice will help you and your family navigate life and financial-planning issues. Get your notebook ready; you're going to need it as you think about the information in these pages.

—W. THOMAS (TOM) MATTHEWS, RETIRED PRESIDENT OF SMITH BARNEY GLOBAL PRIVATE CLIENT GROUP, EMERITUS CHAIRMAN OF THE CONGRESSIONAL MEDAL OF HONOR FOUNDATION

| | | | | | | | | | |

By focusing his clients on the "supporting role" that wealth plays in the meaning of life, Chris Poch has wisely navigated clients through unpredictable yet regular bouts of turmoil in the financial markets. In *Money and Meaning*, Mr. Poch has crafted a roadmap, a rulebook, and a scoreboard for the management of wealth in the service of life's greater goals. He has provided a benefit to all who, in the here and now, are looking for concrete steps to become process-driven, long-term investors.

In reflecting on my experience as a trustee and investor and my time spent in the investment management world, I only wish I had this book to send to my younger self in 1987 at the outset of my investment journey. Chris Poch reminds us to start with the most elemental (budget and save) then craft specifics on how to organize our views against specific actions. He then guides the reader on how to evaluate and retain the spectrum of professionals who will help get them to their destination.

Trust—it is indeed the coin of the realm. Trust in your values, in your goals, in evidence to track progress, and in those enlisted to advise you. *Money and Meaning* is a lucid, tested, and structured guide for getting there.

—CHARLES L. CARROLL, TREASURER OF THE BOARD OF
TRUSTEES AT THE BURKE FOUNDATION, RETIRED DEPUTY
CHAIRMAN AT LAZARD ASSET MANAGEMENT

PREFACE

In 2016, *Managing Your Wealth: A Must-Read for Affluent Families* was published. The content came from articles written for friends and family; they were brief, and many were organized like a checklist. The book contained advice for those who want control over their wealth, including what to do and how to do it. This book is written with ten years more experience and explores how money plays a supporting role as we seek meaning in life.

The most important message I hope to convey in this book is that when managing wealth and money, remember that the ultimate goal is peace of mind. Financial independence is an important part of the journey, and financial assets are tools that enable us to accomplish personal goals. However, caring for family, friends, and community is the highest and best use of wealth, not accumulating money for money's sake.

This book offers ways to approach managing wealth, managing money, and managing family transitions that accompany affluence. Managing wealth has always been more than managing money. To paraphrase Roy Disney: when your values are clear, decision-making is easy. The goal of this book is to reinforce the values that should guide managing wealth in order to make decisions easier.

In this book, you will find perspectives, strategies, and tactics relating to life, wealth, and investing. Before we start at the beginning, we will begin with the end in mind. None of us will be here forever, and among the greatest gifts to leave behind are (1) a sense of gratitude and (2) having one's financial affairs and an estate plan in good order.

To set the framework, it may be beneficial to understand my background. What follows are a few stories that shaped my views and the advice I offer.

Promethium Advisors

After forty years of advising clients as an employee of large wealth-management firms, in 2024, I decided to open an independent advisory firm. One that provides the intimate service and type of common-sense advice I want for myself, my family, and my friends. We focus on the areas we feel are most important and do not try to be everything to everyone. We promise exceptional service, communicate candidly, and pursue compounded, after-tax investment results.

I have always enjoyed the psychic rewards of helping people navigate complex issues to achieve peace of mind and attain financial independence. This is the ethos of Promethium Advisors. We hire people who are unusually committed to delivering exceptional client service and reward our team according to merit, not tenure or title. Being unconstrained by internal business-unit conflicts is a clear win for our clients.

When managing wealth, we adhere to many of the tried-and-true principles. However, to manage taxable, multi-generational money well, one must be willing to be a little different and go beyond offering recommendations that ignore taxes. That can mean having a longer-term investment horizon, being a little more conservative, being a little more tax-sensitive, and focusing on cumulative, after-tax investment results. Smaller companies can do things that are more difficult for larger organizations.

Managing Wealth Is a Serious Business

This book will tell the reader how we at Promethium Advisors manage our financial affairs and those of our clients. After doing this for forty years, I have a view about how most wealthy people should want their financial affairs handled. We help clients understand how to structure and deploy assets to draw families together, not drive them apart. We show them how to transfer wealth without entirely ceding control, and we help them equip heirs to make good choices. None of this is easy.

When it comes to investing assets for multi-generational families, we adhere to a few timeless principles. Once wealthy, families don't need to be twice as rich, they just never want to be half as rich. Owning the latest high-flying stock is great fodder for cocktail conversation, but what really counts is whether or not you make enough money to enable quality education for grandchildren and, if there is enough, endow hospitals and universities.

Managing Assets like Our Own

Promethium Advisors has adopted the investment approach favored by the truly affluent. In later chapters, I will go into detail about how we categorize investing for purpose and time horizons: liquidity, lifestyle, and legacy. To facilitate lifestyle, our core investments are in financially strong, high-quality companies with moderate debt, loyal customers, and rising free cash flow. The preferred outcome is steadily increasing income and moderate volatility.

Unlike most wealth managers, who define risk as volatility, we define risk as permanent loss of capital. We prefer to follow mentors such as Warren Buffett and Charlie Munger, who got rich not by taking more risk but by avoiding risk, being prepared, and, occasionally, being unconventional.

PART I

MANAGING
WEALTH

A Day to Remember

"There appears to be a large imbalance between sell orders and buy orders." I was driving to work early one October Monday morning. The prior Friday, the market had fallen 108 points, or about 5 percent. A radio announcer was describing the plunging Asian markets and predicting a much lower New York Stock Exchange opening.[1] I had read *Barron's* and the Sunday newspapers over the weekend, but no one had any idea what was about to occur that day.

When the market closed six and a half hours later on October 19, 1987, the Dow Jones Industrial Average had plunged 22.7 percent, the single largest one-day drop in history. During the day, the stock prices on our Quotron machines were running hours behind, and the actual prices of some "blue-chip" stocks were 30–50 percent different from what we saw blinking on our screens. Companies, clients, and brokers went bankrupt. Things were so dire, one client in Miami went into his Merrill Lynch broker's office and shot two employees, killing one, before shooting himself, committing suicide.[2]

Lessons Learned

Since then, I have lived through at least four cataclysmic "panics": the 1998 LTCM implosion,[3] the 9/11/2001 terrorist

---

1   Donald Bernhardt and Marshall Eckblad, "Stock Market Crash of 1987," Federal Reserve History, November 22, 2013, https://www.federalreservehistory.org/essays/stock-market-crash-of-1987.

2   Barry Bearak, "Stock Market Loser Kills Brokerage Manager, Self in Shooting Rampage," *Los Angeles Times*, October 27, 1987, https://www.latimes.com/archives/la-xpm-1987-10-27-mn-16905-story.html.

3   Paul Stonham, "Too Close to the Hedge: The Case of Long Term Capital Management LP: Part One: Hedge Fund Analytics," *European Management Journal* 17, no. 3 (June 1999): 282–289, https://doi.org/10.1016/S0263-2373(99)00007-9.

attacks,[4] the 2008 Lehman Bros.–led Great Financial Crisis,[5] and the COVID-induced collapse in 2020.[6] Each was described by the media as "unprecedented." What they all had in common was a big increase in stocks prior to the collapse and few investors saw it coming.

I learned an important lesson after "Black Monday" in 1987— never risk all your capital. Keep some cash on hand, and after a calamity hits, don't wait too long to re-enter the markets. The sun will always shine again, and capitalism will thrive again.

I also learned that as vital to our lives as financial security is, there is more to life than money. It was then, at age twenty-five, that I decided to spend the next what is now approaching forty years helping clients see that they do not need to "beat the market" to win at life. As I learned more, I discovered those who do not stretch to do "the best" often do. More importantly, those who do not over prioritize money tend to live better lives.

The stock market crash of 1987, the single worst day in stock market history, led to the lessons I attempt to relay in this book, *Money and Meaning: What I've Learned from Advising the Very Wealthy.*

---

4 David S. Cloud and Neil King, "Terrorists Destroy World Trade Center, Hit Pentagon in Raid with Hijacked Jets: Death Toll, Source of Devastating Attacks Remain Unclear; U.S. Vows Retaliation as Attention Focuses on bin Laden," *The Wall Street Journal* 238, no. 51 (September 12, 2001): A1, https://www.wsj.com/public/resources/documents/wsj-paper-09122001.pdf.

5 Peter Gratton, "Stock Market Crash of 2008," Investopedia, last updated November 21, 2024, https://www.investopedia.com/articles/economics/09/subprime-market-2008.asp.

6 Liz Frazier, "The Coronavirus Crash of 2020, and the Investing Lesson It Taught Us," *Forbes*, last updated April 14, 2022, https://www.forbes.com/sites/lizfrazierpeck/2021/02/11/the-coronavirus-crash-of-2020-and-the-investing-lesson-it-taught-us/.

Wealth Principles

Money is not wealth, and neither money nor wealth brings happiness or meaning to life. Our goal in life should be the peace of mind that comes from being content with who we are and what we have. Understanding how to accumulate "enough" wealth to gain peace of mind is the objective of this book.

In this section, you will learn how to assemble a team of advisors, how to get good service, and how to be a good client. I offer suggestions on how to involve your family, make sure your estate is in good order, and inform and prepare your heirs.

Having wealth entails ongoing responsibilities. The principles that follow provide a digestible roadmap that allows you to understand what to do, why it should be done, and, in the process, how to find meaning in life regardless of how much or how little money you have.

People with wealth know that in order to accumulate, keep, and sustain wealth over generations, you must first learn to budget and save. This applies to people just starting out as well as those with hundreds of millions of dollars.

CHAPTER 1

|||||||||||

BUDGET, SAVE, AND INVEST

"No mo' FOMO."[7]

My youngest daughter is now in her late twenties and lives on the West Coast. When she got her first job, we sat down together and mapped out how to budget her modest salary. We allowed for taxes, signed up for a 401(k), and set up an automated payroll deduction for a small amount to be invested. She invested her monthly savings in an after-tax investment account at a well-known mutual-fund company. We agreed that when she received a raise, part of the increase would go into her after-tax investment account. It didn't need to be a lot; it just needed to be something.

---

7   FOMO is an acronym that means "fear of missing out."

Those susceptible to influencers make
others rich, not themselves happy.

Ever since then, she and I have had a video call the first week in February when she fills out her tax return. The first year, I did most of the talking as she input the numbers. The second year, she did more of the talking, and I answered a few questions. In recent years, she tells me how much her balance has grown and the amount of dividend income on which she pays tax. It has gone up every year. We now have the annual call for my benefit, not hers.

"When outgo exceeds income, your upkeep
becomes your downfall."
—*Jim Rohn*

After her first year, I told her, "You may never be rich, but you will absolutely be financially secure." Periodically, she will relay to me a conversation she had with friends who live paycheck to paycheck, carry balances on their credit cards, and have had no guidance about financial stewardship. By that I mean many people, young and old, do not realize how much they end up paying in interest expenses. They are seduced into thinking they are "smart" for choosing a credit card that offers more reward points, even if it has a high annual fee or charges a 24 percent annual interest rate. She has become the finance teacher for her friends. Many of her friends make more money than her but have less savings.

All families, whether with a net worth of $50 million or $50,000, do their children a disservice if they fail to emphasize the critical step of budgeting and saving early in their children's lives. Teaching them how to manage their financial affairs has an extremely high return on time.

Income minus expenses = $1, happiness

Income minus expenses = -$1, misery

In my opinion, learning this life lesson is as important to your child's future as where they go to college and almost as important as the spouse they select. Fidelity, good communication, and alignment on managing finances are the top three contributors to a happy marriage.

Teaching my daughter the principles of living below her means and saving every month by showing her the tools and giving her the confidence that it will work has paid off in spades. Her success may be the highlight of my financial advisory career. It is not hard, but you need a willing pupil who will trust your advice and follow through.

Do the same for your children and grandchildren. It may quietly be the single most important lesson you teach them and the crowning achievement of your financial legacy.

"Now that you have learned how to budget and save, any chance you can lease out the empty office building we own?"

SUMMARY

1. Budgeting means planning in advance what your expenditures will be. When you plan to save, you can see why you did or did not and know what changes, if any, are needed.

2. Wealth and peace of mind are accumulated in "after tax" accounts. Invest a little every month outside your retirement plans to be on the road to financial independence.

3. Knowing you are doing all the right things well before you hit your wealth-accumulation goals should provide confidence and satisfaction.

Next Chapter

1. The next chapter emphasizes the importance of taking the long view with your family's assets and, by your example, educating future generations to do the same.

2. Conservative financial management and maintaining a modest lifestyle will help the generations to come understand how to enjoy the family's good fortune and avoid having it end with them.

3. A few words of caution regarding alternative investments and how to improve your odds of understanding what you are investing in.

CHAPTER 2

||||||||||

HOW TO MANAGE YOUR FAMILY'S FORTUNE

The single most important factor in successfully managing your family's fortune is to have the proper mindset. Understand that a family's time horizon for financial growth may be decades or longer and that growth takes time and requires patience.

Next, the primary objective is to earn "real returns." That is to say that returns over the rate of inflation and after taxes are key. Some only include inflation when defining "real returns," but I include taxes. For those of us who live in the real world, this is the minimum threshold. So, for example, if inflation is 3 percent, and you pay another 2 percent in taxes, you need to earn at least 5 percent to "break even." Anything above 5 percent is, by my definition, a "real return" and increases your purchasing power. With these two guideposts to frame our thinking, and before we dive into ways to maximize wealth, we pause for a moment of introspection to ask, "How much is enough?"

"Am I Enough?"

A man in his early sixties sold his company for an amount that would be life changing for almost anyone. He asked a friend of mine, who was a counselor to wealthy families, "Do I have enough?" My friend paused, then he responded, "I don't know, are *you* enough?" My friend was asking, indirectly, whether the man was happy with who he was as a person, regardless of the amount of money he had.

I overheard this story almost thirty years ago, and it has stayed with me. The moral of the story is that we can be very happy without a lot of material wealth if we are happy with who we are inside and how we treat other people. I will not attempt to provide insight into attaining internal peace but will start from the perspective that peace of mind is the ultimate goal, with financial independence as one stop along the way.

In some cases, once a person hits their goal, achieves power and fame, or makes a lot of money, their human nature kicks in, and it still isn't enough.

Focus On the Right Things

||||||

"Baseball is 90 percent mental.
The other half is physical."
—Yogi Berra

||||||

Yogi Berra's quote also applies to wealth and investing. When you get the mindset right, behavior comes naturally. Our investment behavior, much more than our investment decisions, determines our financial outcomes and happiness.

Avoid Permanent Losses

Preserving capital is the first step toward growing it. For a family's wealth and purchasing power to grow, you do not need to "beat the market" every year. Steady compounding by owning growth and income assets should get you there.

Some focus too heavily on the amount their account goes up or down each month and reducing volatility. For most people, it only matters what happens over the course of five to ten years. Investors know prices go up and down. That is not a risk—that is a fact. Instead, it is better to define risk as the possibility that if the price of something goes down, it will never recover. That is a permanent loss of capital, and we want to minimize that risk. Make every effort to avoid large losses so that your wealth can compound at attractive rates over time. The power of compounding is, as Einstein is credited with saying, "The eighth wonder of the world."

1. **Long-term.** I believe the surest path to generating attractive investment returns is to maintain a long-term focus. This allows you to patiently wait for the realization of value without being swayed by market volatility or news headlines. It also reduces portfolio turnover, which can detract from returns.

2. **Cash-flow orientation.** Invest with a margin of safety, seek rising cash flow, and resist the "fear of missing out" syndrome. Over a five-to-ten-year period, avoiding large selloffs normally more than makes up for not owning the "hot" sector. When stock market valuations appear "high," do not underestimate the benefits of holding cash despite the short-term drag on performance. Cash gives a host of choices. When you buy assets with the intent to own them for a long time, it reduces the risk of buying and selling at the wrong time and, if you make a profit, the cost of taxes owed on gains—all of which can detract from wealth accumulation.

3. **Diversification.** Once you are wealthy, the goal is to stay wealthy. Owning an array of assets that generate cash on a regular basis minimizes the risk of unexpected events—market crashes, health problems, loss of employment—impairing your lifestyle and future. Stocks, bonds, cash, and real estate are the core four assets. Your decisions to buy and sell assets should be based on economic cycles, not short-term stock market moves. However, diversification does not guarantee a profit nor protect against a loss.

4. **Fundamentals count.** Finding a great business at the right price is rare, and when you do, you want to own it

in size and be slow to sell. You cannot own too much of a great company that has strong financials, a high return on capital, and loyal customers.

5. **Ownership orientation.** The way to maintain purchasing power after taxes, inflation, and expenses is to own assets that will produce rising income streams at attractive rates. With this mindset, you can withstand interim volatility. In other words, buy income-producing stocks and real estate. Over time, stocks are a better hedge against inflation than bonds and provide a greater opportunity to achieve attractive absolute returns.

6. **Partners and aligned interests.** Seek out situations where the principals are co-invested alongside you, will enjoy proportional benefit, and pay the same fees. If it is good for the goose, it should be good for the gander.

Job Number 1—Allocating Capital

Managing your family's fortune is like being the chair of the board. Your two primary jobs are to determine strategy and find the right people. Your strategy is what you want to be invested in. Your second job is to hire the right people to do the first job for you. The more you can allocate to ownership of assets (stocks, real estate, or private businesses), preferably cash-generating assets that are likely to increase, the better.

Preferred Asset Characteristics

1. **Strong balance sheet.** Companies with strong financials, moderate debt, and the ability to access and deploy capital during times of economic stress are preferred. When that happens, they tend to grow market share and

thrive coming out of recessions. Their ability to generate high, free cash flow enables them the flexibility to make investments to improve service and quality, lower costs, and secure acquisitions.

2. **High returns on invested capital.** Industries that do not require continual capital investments in order to grow are where the greatest earnings-compounding opportunities exist.

3. **Loyal customers.** Great companies have loyal customers who are not lured away by a temporarily discounted price. Loyal customers know they receive value at higher price points.

4. **Essential products and services.** It is exciting to buy shares in the next blockbuster drug or disruptive technology company, but they don't always work out as well as planned. I prefer to own companies that sell products and services that people need in both good and bad economic times.

5. **Leadership in a growing industry.** When an industry expands, its leaders often enjoy a disproportionate share of the growth, and when it shrinks, the smaller players are at greater risk of going out of business.

6. **Sustainable competitive advantages.** Lower costs, better technology, patent protection, as well as reputations for service and quality are all reasons great franchises have staying power.

7. **Trustworthy people and aligned incentives.** Seek to invest in companies whose managers have high levels of integrity, are excellent operators, and have proven records of profitable capital allocation.

Avoid Overdiversification

Virtually all large banks and brokerage firms recommend owning dozens of asset classes.[8] In the last forty years, many studies have shown that the broader your investable universe is, the more diversified you should be. Other studies have come to a different conclusion. They found that as the "quality" of the investable universe goes up, the need to diversify to reduce risk goes down.[9] Said differently, the riskier the investment, the greater the diversification required to mitigate that risk.

Many asset-allocation models recommend small amounts, 1–2 percent, be invested in sub-asset categories, such as mid-cap growth, emerging-market fixed income, mortgages, high-yield corporate bonds, commodities, or hedge funds.

The percent allocations can be so small one might logically ask whether they will impact the results (almost assuredly not), and if not, why bother? Some have suggested this practice might be due to the wealth-management firm's desire to allocate clients' assets to countries where the firm solicits corporate or government business and distributes products.

Regardless, the more complex your balance sheet gets, the more reliant on advisors you become, but don't be seduced by slick presentations. My advice is to diversify—up to a point. As much as you can, keep it simple.

---

8   By asset classes, I mean stocks, bonds, and cash as well as the subdivisions of each—large-, small-, and medium-capitalization stocks; international and emerging-market stocks; value and growth stocks; government, corporate, and municipal bonds; private equity; private credit; hedge funds; venture capital funds; commodity funds; mutual funds; and exchange-traded funds, just to name a few.

9   John L. Evans and Stephen H. Archer, "Diversification and the Reduction of Dispersion: An Empirical Analysis," *The Journal of Finance* 23, no. 5 (December 1968): 761–767, https://doi.org/10.2307/2325905.

Should I Just Buy an Index Fund?

For small investors with modest tax bills, the answer is yes. An index fund is a low-cost mutual fund invented in the 1970s. The stocks in the fund mimic stock market indexes. Index funds are a wonderful, low-cost way for investors to gain broad exposure to the prosperity of ownership. It is estimated that passive index funds have grown to nearly 60 percent of the equity market.[10]

However, indiscriminately buying more of the companies whose prices have gone up the most, irrespective of valuation, sets up two problematic assumptions: (1) that their growth will go on forever, and (2) that everyone who invests in index funds actually earns the published returns.

Proponents correctly point out that passive portfolios have outperformed more than two-thirds of actively managed US equity portfolios over the last twenty years.[11] What is under-reported is that, at the same time, the average equity index investor also underperformed the index by a wide margin.[12] Higher investment-management and advisory fees are not the main reason the average investor's actual results are less than the published performance of the funds they own—it is the investor's behavior that is to blame.

---

10   "Mutual Funds 2030," PricewaterhouseCoopers, accessed June 20, 2025, https://www.pwc.com/us/en/industries/financial-services/library/mutual-fund-outlook.html.

11   Murray Coleman, "Active Fund Managers vs. Indexes: Analyzing SPIVA Scorecards," Tax Fund Advisors, last updated April 15, 2025, https://www.ifa.com/articles/spiva-report-active-vs-passive.

12   Murray Coleman, "Dalbar QAIB 2025: Investors Are Still Their Own Worst Enemies," Index Fund Advisors, last updated May 7, 2025, https://www.ifa.com/articles/understanding-investor-behavior-portfolio-performance.

Market Timing

History shows that investors tend to pour more money into the stock market after several years of strong equity performance. Investors then, after markets decline, lose confidence and withdraw capital near market bottoms.

Legendary investor Stanley Druckenmiller observed that a buy and hold strategy "beats trying to time the market because 85 percent of people do worse than random."[13]

Studies by Dalbar over the last thirty years show the average mutual-fund investor earns about 50–60 percent of the index.[14] Studies also show, year after year, most people don't have the stomach to be responsible for making economic decisions when the market sells off 20–30 percent.[15]

For most, it is better to outsource the day-to-day decisions to financial professionals who specialize in investing client assets. Advisors may not outperform an index after fees, but they generally do better than the investor would on their own.[16]

---

13 Stanley Druckenmiller, "DealBook Conference 2015—The Other Investors' Perspective," moderated by Andrew Ross Sorkin, interview, posted November 3, 2015, by New York Times Events, YouTube, 24:48, https://www.youtube.com/watch?v=loYjPekmccs.

14 Coleman, "Dalbar QAIB 2025."

15 Brad M. Barber and Terrance Odean, "The Behavior of Individual Investors," *Handbook of the Economics of Finance* 2, part B (2013): 1540, https://doi.org/10.1016/B978-0-44-459406-8.00022-6.

16 Francis M. Kinniry Jr. et al., *Putting a Value on Your Value: Quantifying Vanguard Advisor's Alpha,* Vanguard (July 2022), https://corporate.vanguard.com/content/dam/corp/articles/pdf/putting_value_on_your_value_quantifying_vanguard_advisors_alpha.pdf.

A Cautionary Word on Investing in "Alternatives"

It is standard for most financial professionals to recommend "alternative investments." Advisors are taught that this asset class lowers risk and increases returns. Though there are innumerable studies that support this assertion, in my opinion, the conclusions, unexamined, can create a false sense of security for five reasons.

1. **Survivor bias.** The indexes most often cited to represent the asset classes disproportionately suffer from survivor bias. Survivor bias occurs when funds that do poorly, lose money, or close are omitted. This leaves just the better performing funds in historical calculations, overstating investors' actual experiences.[17]

2. **Lack of independent valuations.** The majority of the valuations, upon which fees and returns are calculated, are not conducted by independent entities.

3. **Infrequent and delayed valuations.** Some valuations of illiquid investments, such as private equity and venture capital, are done annually, semi-annually, or quarterly. If the general partner values the asset at cost for a few years, it artificially dampens volatility. Others, such as fund-of-funds partnership structures, are routinely delayed (also referred to as "stale") and often artificially compress volatility.

4. **Unknown leverage.** The amount of leverage employed at any time is difficult or near impossible to know and can creep in, potentially boosting short-term returns while adding risk without the investor knowing.

---

17   "Biases of Hedge Fund Data," ABC Quant, accessed June 20, 2025, https://www.abcquant.com/biases-of-hedge-fund-data.

5. **Dispersion between best and worst funds.** The difference between the best and worst performing "alternative asset" funds is large.[18] The odds of an investor with less than $500 million getting into the "best performing funds" are effectively zero, unless by investing in a fund-of-funds partnership. Funds of funds carry incremental fees, which materially reduce the investor's return. The lower-returning fund of funds "performance" is not included in the index "average" returns.

The statement that adding "alternatives" lowers volatility can be true, but not always. Most "alternative" investments use some sort of leverage and have higher volatility than implied. Due to infrequent pricing, there appears to be less volatility. The return patterns vary massively when you invest in venture capital, private equity, hedge funds, private credit, or real estate.[19] It would be a mistake to conclude there is less volatility just because your statement shows the same value for several quarters or a couple years.

Another statement that needs to be taken with a grain of salt is that an allocation to "alternative investments" is "smart" because they are good diversifiers. Again, unexamined, this statement presumes all diversification is good. Whether the new asset will lower volatility or return more than what you would have made by owning common stocks cannot be known in advance. It is true alternative investments can make money

---

18 Andrew Snyder et al., "Performance Dispersion in Alternative Asset Classes," CAIS, November 18, 2022, https://www.caisgroup.com/articles/performance-dispersion-in-alternative-asset-classes.

19 Jon Luskin, "The Diversification Myth of Alternative Investments: How Illiquidity Is Mistaken for Low Correlation," *Jon Luskin* (blog), February 1, 2022, https://jonluskin.com/the-diversification-myth-of-alternative-investments/.

and may lower statement volatility. However, it would be a mistake to assume that all of the "alternative investments" you are likely to be shown will have the same risk and return patterns of the recent past.

Whatever you decide about investing in "alternative" investments, be sure your economic interests are aligned with whomever is recommending illiquid investments that carry leverage. Be sure that the placement fees and seven-to-ten-year revenue stream to the advisor do not cloud anyone's judgment about future expectations.[20]

---

20 Kate Dore, "Some Advisors Are Flocking to Alternative Investments, Survey Finds. What Investors Need to Know," CNBC, last updated June 27, 2023, https://www.cnbc.com/2023/06/27/heres-what-to-know-about-alternative-investments-before-buying.html.

WHY ME, WHY NOW?

The next time someone recommends an "alternative invest-ment," ask yourself, *Why is this being offered to me, a relatively small investor? Why doesn't the selling sponsor save themselves the hassle of having hundreds of small, limited partners rather than a couple large, sophisticated ones? If the investment is so good, why doesn't the $50 billion Harvard Endowment or the $500 billion California pension fund want more of it?* The answer could be because there are no more large fund buyers on those terms or at that price.

SELECTIVITY IS KEY

Some funds do quite well because they benefit from lever-age, prudent management, and a long-term holding period. However, making a high-risk or highly leveraged investment, or speculating on market moves with investor capital with a "heads I win, tails you lose" fee arrangement, can lead to differ-ent outcomes for the general partner and the investor. When things go as planned, the investor does well, and the hedge fund, venture capital, and private equity managers get rich. When things do not go as planned, the investor loses money, and the general partners open a new fund. A lot of the products offered today remind me of the question posed by Fred Schwed Jr., "Where are the customers' yachts?"[21]

---

21   Fred Schwed Jr., *Where Are the Customers' Yachts?: Or A Good Hard Look at Wall Street* (Hoboken, N.J.: Wiley, 2006).

Thoughtful Investing in Private Businesses

Co-investing directly in private businesses that distribute cash flow from day one can be an attractive alternative to the mega-sized "blind pool" fund-of-funds partnership structure. To the extent possible, be sure the person recommending the investment personally has sufficient skin in the game. With all non-tradeable investments: caveat emptor, or, as the wise carpenter says, "Measure twice, cut once."

Job Number 2—Identifying Advisors

In order to capture attractive returns, investors need to have the conviction to remain invested through the inevitable downturns. If you have what it takes and are among the top 10–15 percent of investors who are able to ignore large market declines, do it yourself. If not, hire a firm or an advisor who meets the criteria to do it for you.

Therefore, the second primary job of managing your family's fortune is to select a team. Finding a Senior Strategic Advisor to coordinate and communicate with your tax, trust, insurance, banking, and investing teams is ideal. The next chapter offers a step-by-step guide for those in search of a wealth advisor.

Summary

1. Overseeing your family's fortune requires a balance of vision and patience. Investing for returns that will exceed the negative effects of inflation, taxes, and expenses will ensure your standard of living improves. Conservative growth gets you there.

2. Focus on how much money is accumulated in dollars over time. Average annual returns sell financial products. Compound returns generate dollars to live on and invest for the future.

3. Avoid the lure of the promises of high returns from high-risk ventures. Shiny objects are appealing but often don't pan out.

Next Chapter

1. The next chapter offers thoughts on how you can improve your chances of getting a qualified wealth advisor at a firm that has the optimal combination of services, skills, and expertise.

2. The first step in selecting the right advisor is to know the core services you need and how you prefer to engage. Most financial providers have similar sets of products and services. Learn the questions to ask to home in on what counts for you.

3. Trust between the client and the advisor is paramount. Seek evidence of the results of the promises made by the companies and people you are considering.

CHAPTER 3

IN SEARCH OF A WEALTH ADVISOR

STURGEON'S LAW

My father-in-law was a world-renowned endocrinologist, genet-icist, author, and lecturer. He and I often discussed science, statistics, probabilities, and human behavior. Or, to be more precise, he spoke, and I listened.

He once observed, "A random patient with a random condi-tion who sees a random doctor may end up with a random diagnosis." The same is true for wealth advisors. Sturgeon's Law may be a little crass, but it drives home a point. Theodore Sturgeon, a science-fiction writer, was asked why the quality of science-fiction writing was so low. He responded, "Ninety percent of everything is crud, so why should science fiction be any different?"[22]

---

22 James Gunn, "Addendum: Sturgeon's Law," *The New York Review of Science Fiction* 85 (September 1995), https://faculty.college.emory.edu/sites/weeks/misc/slaw.html.

I don't know if 90 percent is the right number, but, broadly speaking, in my experience, it is not far off. Odds are fair that the people reading this book are in the top 5 percent of education, affluence, and discernment. Accordingly, the wealth advisors who service this small group are likely in the top half of quality and knowledge. Take it from me, even among the top half of investment advisors, the difference in the client experience between the top 15 percent and the rest is significant.[23]

Know Thyself

I imagine that many people have asked themselves, "How does one select a wealth advisor?" From forty years of observations, I have a good idea of what most clients want and need.

The most important step is to first understand that your own behavior will drive your results. Twenty to thirty years down the road, your net worth could be double or half depending on your selection process. Saving, patience, and persistence are the most critical factors to accumulating and compounding wealth. Having an advisor who reinforces those behaviors is an essential part of the recipe for success.

Know What to Look For

1. **Write down what you want.** Start with the types of services you need and the relationship you want. Do you require financial planning, estate planning, or trust

---

23   This claim is from both personal experience and the Pareto Principle; "Pareto Charts & 80-20 Rule," CEC Academy, NSW Government, accessed June 20, 2025, https://www.cec.health.nsw.gov.au/CEC-Academy/quality-improvement-tools/pareto-charts.

services? Will you need insurance, philanthropic, or tax planning? In the important areas, ask to see sample work. The more complex your situation is, the more effort may be required to find the right fit.

2. **Client experience.** Great client experiences from financial institutions are increasingly rare. Write down your service expectations for your wealth advisory team. Note the things you prefer and what is missing from your current provider. Look for a system that explains what you will receive, tells you how frequently services will be provided, and provides examples. If the service is "fully customized to each client," that might indicate there is no system.

3. **Investment products.** Do you want a one-stop shop for investments, insurance, home loans, and credit cards? Do you prefer providers with focused expertise? Do you want an advisor who selects a money manager with an audited, SEC-compliant track record to buy and sell securities?[24]

4. **Ongoing education.** Learning about financial management is a lifelong process, and the best companies have programs that enable it. Make sure your advisor has the content and disposition to help you learn more.

HONEST AND EARNEST

Most people simply need an honest person who will guide them on the basics: saving, long-term investing, and sticking with a

---

24 U.S. Securities and Exchange Commission, "SEC Proposes Rules to Modernize and Enhance Information Reported by Investment Companies and Investment Advisers," press release, May 20, 2015, https://www.sec.gov/newsroom/press-releases/2015-95.

sound plan. Understanding that stocks have historically out-performed bonds, investing through dollar cost averaging, and spending less than they make will get most people to financial independence.

For the family with significant assets, better advice can make a meaningful difference. It is worth going the extra mile to find a well-qualified wealth advisor with a thoughtful service system. Put in the effort now. You will benefit many times over in the future.

WHO DO YOU KNOW?

A common way to find potential wealth advisors is to ask friends who they use. These generally pass the first test: are they trust-worthy? Remember, however, that friends' opinions reflect their own preferences and experiences, which may be different from yours.

Have your checklist ready:

- Which services are provided, how frequently, by whom, and who initiates?
- Who takes your call on weekends, and when can you expect that call to be returned?
- Request tangible samples of work product that meet the complexity of your needs.
- Request a copy of their client-satisfaction survey results.
- Request a copy of their investment commentary and results.

Business Models

The business model of the firm you select will have a significant impact on the advice you are given, products you are sold, and services you are offered. Advisors are trained to sell the products in which their company specializes, and the service is dictated by the business practices of the company.

The following are common business models:

- **Large banks.** Offer a broad array of products and are preferred by clients with modest assets who prioritize choice and convenience. Brand implies permanence and safety. Staff tend to be less experienced, and the number of clients per person tends to be higher.
- **Brokerage firms.** Structured to serve every client segment: corporations, municipalities, non-profits, and individuals. Asset allocation and product recommendations are generally centralized and usually skew heavily toward "alternative" investments. Advisor experience varies from best in class to trainees.
- **Trust companies.** Almost always attached to a bank or asset-management firm. Provide administrators to follow trust instructions and legal requirements. Investment results have historically been weak.[25]
- **Registered investment advisors (RIAs).** Independent fiduciaries with fewer conflicts of interest than registered reps of broker-dealers. Brokers are allowed to sell recom-

---

25 Jennifer Strachan, "IAM Forensic Service Case Studies: When Things Go Wrong with Investment Portfolios Held in Trust," IAM Advisory, November 16, 2020, https://iamadvisory.com/thinking/news-insight/insights/when-things-go-wrong-portfolios-held-in-trust/; Jeffrey L. Crown, "How to Improve Trust Returns and Reduce Conflicts with Total Return Trusts," Trust Lawyer LLC, accessed June 20, 2025, http://trustlawyer.com/articles/articles-professionals/how-improve-trust-returns-and-reduce-conflicts-total-return-trusts.

mendations that are "suitable" but not necessarily "the best available." RIAs use external providers for custody, statements, trading, and tax reporting. Quality of advice varies widely from annuity salespeople to family-office providers.

Know Your Advisor

Most wealth advisors do the best job they can with the training they received and recommend the products their company sells. Advisors at mutual-fund companies extol the virtues of and recommend funds and exchange-traded funds (ETFs). People trained at insurance companies recommend insurance solutions; those at banks recommend banking products. Firms with investment-banking relationships in recent years have increased their focus on "alternative investments," many, coincidentally, managed by their investment banks' private equity clients.

It is for this reason that understanding an advisor's background will provide insight into their experiences, biases, and inclinations. It is said surgeons "heal with steel" and real estate developers "borrow and build." If what you really need are dress shoes but find yourself in a sporting goods store, you may walk out with a pair of sneakers or cleats. Know before you go.

In large measure, your experience rests in the hands of the advisory team you select. Determining an advisor's level of skill is difficult even for experienced clients. Skip the internal titles. Many industry certifications are robust and indicate mastery of information but do not indicate knowing when and how to apply it. When interviewing candidates, ask yourself:

- How well do they listen?
- Do they ask good questions?
- Do they use jargon or speak plainly?
- Do they write things down?
- How will they help me learn?

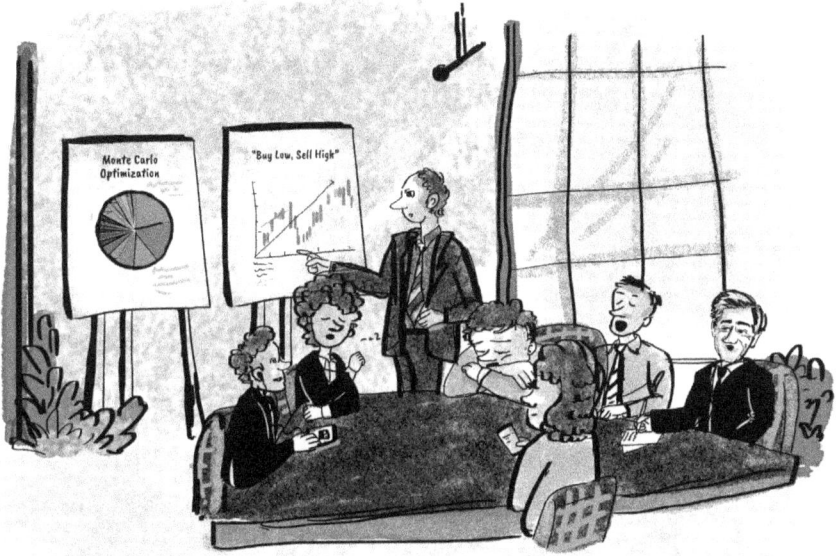

"How well do they listen? Do they use jargon or speak plainly? Do they ask good questions?"

PREFERRED: ORIGINAL THINKING, VERIFIED RESULTS

Some advisors have authored market commentaries. Much of the investment commentary attributed to investment advisors is actually ghostwritten articles with the advisor's firm's logo affixed. Even fewer have third-party audited investment results.

If there is an audited, SEC-compliant track record available, ask to review it.

Understanding the Nuances

Now that you have the checklist and questions, let's go a little deeper before you interview the candidates.

- **Investment, income tax, trust and estate law, insurance.** The wealth advisory team you select should be knowledgeable enough to advise at your level of complexity. They should understand all recommendations regarding income tax, estate tax, insurance, and philanthropy.
- **Desired service level.** Not every client needs the "platinum" package, but no one wants an advisor who calls to read a prepared sales script from a memo drafted by the "product of the month" team back at the home office. Probe how proactive your wealth management team will be and how they plan to interact with your other advisors.
- **Compensation drives behavior.** Does the advisor's compensation vary based on asset mix or product? Products that have fees paid directly to the advisor, such as alternative investments, structured notes, and insurance, are usually not included in recurring monthly fees. If advisor fees can be layered on top of other fees, be leery.
- **Sales.** Advisors who are paid based on product sales tend to contact clients to sell to them. Conversely, some advisors paid on recurring fees don't engage enough.
- **Satisfaction.** Firms that pay employees based on client satisfaction and do not have sales quotas tend to attract employees who are service-oriented. Many clients prefer that.

*When your economic interest diverges
from your advisor's economic interest,
the recommendations usually follow the
economic interest of the advisor.*

Evaluating Proposals

Most wealth advisory firms' presentations to prospective clients focus on their company, its history, and their products and services. These days, most companies provide similar products and services to some degree. It seems like every proposal lists every imaginable service to every imaginable client segment. Some claim "access to products" due to some special relationship with a vendor. Virtually all claim unique expertise, a number-one ranking, or the most of something in some narrow definition during some period of time.

I asked a former boss at arguably the largest global wealth-management firm if what we were saying was actually true. He said it is if you, "BYOB." When I looked puzzled, he went on to explain that it is true if you "believe your own BS." I have found that many people have talked themselves into believing that their firm offers something truly unique. My response is, "Show me."

At some point, you will receive an investment proposal. Invariably, the proposal will include a combination of investment products with impressive past performances. Know that, in almost all cases, the investment recommendation was selected because it had the highest risk-adjusted past performance and met your objectives. Hence, every proposal will be impressive, and you can never compare apples to apples.

Whether the strategies are likely to work in the future is for you to discern.

PERFORMANCE

Ask how the results were achieved and what the firm was thinking prior to its "outperformance." Why did they take a different view from the consensus? The question to answer is, "Going forward, how likely is it that I would have a similar experience?" Ideally, assuming the time horizon and objectives are similar, clients will experience the same investment results. That is difficult to find and even harder to verify. Make your selection based on an aligned philosophy, process, and framework, not primarily on past performance or price.

"Sometimes you make 300 percent, sometimes 100 percent. You have to take the bad with the good."

When someone doesn't know what qualitative aspects to look for, they might focus on explicit costs. However, be sure to understand why razorblade companies give away razors. Otherwise, you might get nicked.

All-in costs. It is important to know the "all-in" costs and how they might change as the portfolio changes. Some firms state the advisor's fee and omit the underlying product fees, which can double the costs. Others entice prospects by initially recommending very low-cost investment products only to change recommendations down the road. When all is said and done, high-quality wealth-management firms charge between 1 and 2 percent on assets under management.[26] In most relationships above $10 million, fees are less, but the investment mix influences the final number.

Broker, advisor, or fiduciary? Today, an advisor at a Financial Industry Regulatory Authority (FINRA)-regulated broker-dealer operates as both a broker and an "investment advisor representative." RIAs registered solely under the Securities and Exchange Commission (SEC) are only fiduciaries and cannot sell commission-based products.

Avoid the bait and switch. If the proposed fee is below market, ask where and how the firm is making up the difference. High fees reduce your net worth, so avoid them. *However, a rock-bottom fee sentences you to inexperienced staff and call-center–quality service.* Nobody wants that.

---

26 Akhilesh Ganti, "What Is a Brokerage Fee? How Fees Work and Types," Investopedia, last updated October 3, 2024, https://www.investopedia.com/terms/b/brokerage-fee.asp.

Adopt the mindset that you want to get the most value out of your advisor, not pay the least.

Number of Providers

It might be tempting to split your money and invest half with one advisor and the other half with a second to see which advisor "does better." If you hire one investment specialist for real estate and another to manage stocks and bonds, that may be a good idea. However, if you split your money between two advisors that do very similar things, it rarely works out well. Most people want to be important to their advisors to ensure good service and, when possible, to simplify their lives. The more money you have with your advisor, the more important you will be to them.

Avoid Horse Races

Be careful not to set up a performance "horse race" between providers. In order to win the rest of your business, or avoid losing what they have, advisors are motivated to covertly engage in a performance race. Risk seeps into portfolios and is often only understood after unexpected losses.

"It's a mistake for investment management to hire armies of people to make conclusions. Better off to concentrate your decision power in one person... and choose the right person. I don't think it's easy for ordinary people to become great investors."
—Charlie Munger, Vice Chair
of Berkshire Hathaway

Select one. Despite the limitations, I recommend selecting one high-quality firm. Give them the mandate to manage the entire relationship and enlist your tax, insurance, and other advisors to be the "watch dogs." Once a year, ask all your advisors for their opinions of each other. Good advisors will tell you the truth. Weak advisors should be replaced.

Avoid brown paint. To some, this may sound like putting all your eggs in one basket, but I don't see it that way. To me, it is the best way to get accountability. My dad, Robert A. Poch, was a lifelong hardware man. He was fond of saying, "If too many people are mixing the paint, all you end up with is brown paint."

Summary

1. Know what you want and look for evidence to verify the promises of superior service from potential advisors. Most financial advisors are polished and professional, but like every profession, there can be a big difference even among the top 20 percent. It takes effort to parse the differences.

2. Service and communication are key. Request examples, client testimonials, and survey results. This step can reveal a high-touch client experience or a sterile, institutional process.

3. Discern whether your primary advisor has investment skill. Results matter.

Next Chapter

1. Selecting a qualified wealth advisor is key, but it is only part of the job of managing your family's fortune. The next chapter explains that most families need the core four advisors: tax, legal/estate, insurance, and investments.

2. Assembling a group with overlapping knowledge and the ability to work in harmony is critical. Communication between and among your advisors is key.

3. Task one advisor, your Senior Strategic Advisor, with keeping the "to-do" list. This will make everyone's job easier, ensure accountability, and ease interactions.

CHAPTER 4

|||||||||||

HOW TO ASSEMBLE A TEAM OF ADVISORS

How Many People Does It Take to Change a Light Bulb?

In 2001, my family and I moved to Greenwich, Connecticut, and bought a cute 1930s Tudor-style home. One of the early discoveries was that a leak from a small bathroom had seeped through the first-floor ceiling, and repairs would need to be done pronto. We called in a highly recommended tile contractor. After some back and forth, we were told we would also need a plumber and an electrician. We were new in town, and, not knowing anyone, the tile contactor volunteered to be the general contractor, for our convenience. I'll save you the details of the three-month project the real estate broker said would cost $3,000. Our six-by-eight-foot remodeled bathroom cost $30,000. Since then, I have been far more deliberate in assembling teams.

Selecting the right team to advise you on strategic issues is as important to your wealth as your investment selections. This team will usually include a tax professional, an investment advisor, one or more attorneys, and an insurance broker. For this discussion, I will focus on the needs of families with $25 million or more in assets. These usually include multiple homes, trusts, charitable funds, and partnerships, and they are often subject to state taxes in more than one state.

CERTIFIED PUBLIC ACCOUNTANTS (CPAs)

1. **Know what you need.** Do you require financial reports for several entities? Do you have LLCs, trusts, partnerships, scheduled gifts, a family foundation, and business interests in different states? As you add complexity, an understanding of the interrelationships, deductibility, and tax treatments becomes increasingly important.

2. **Aren't all CPAs the same?** Tax laws are the same, and the software that most certified public accountants (CPAs) use is the same. The differentiators are training, professional experience, and familiarity with unique items. Membership in the American Institute of CPAs (AICPA) is a good start. The Personal Financial Specialist designation from the AICPA indicates an additional level of training.

3. **Local firm, boutique, or Big Four?** If your needs are complex, and especially if you are exposed to international tax law, a Big Four firm may be the right option for you.[27] However, most clients will do just fine with regional tax firms. If you are subject to taxes in multiple states, ask about their state and local tax (SALT) capabilities.

---

27 The "Big Four" accounting firms are Deloitte, Ernst & Young (EY), PricewaterhouseCoopers (PwC), and Klynveld Peat Marwick Goerdeler (KPMG), all known for their global presence, extensive service offerings, and auditing of many of the world's largest corporations.

Trust and Estate Attorneys

Most wealthy families need an attorney to discuss large asset purchases and legal structures. For the purpose of this discussion, however, I will focus on the issues regarding estate planning. Among the many considerations when choosing an attorney are state licensing, advanced certifications, and general experience. Participation in the American Bar Association (ABA) on real property or trust and estate law or in the state bar is a good sign. A coveted, peer-awarded designation is Fellow of the American College of Trust and Estate Counsel (ACTEC).

There are many, many excellent attorneys who are not affiliated with these organizations. Some are extremely sophisticated legal generalists, and others are managing partners of white-shoe firms. However, when you evaluate your attorney selection, have a thoughtful process.

Insurance Professionals

Disclaimer: I have been licensed to sell life insurance off and on over the last forty years. The reason being that in order to advise a client to not buy life insurance, one must be licensed to say it. When clients need life insurance, we routinely refer them to professionals with relevant knowledge and experience. I recommend using the same evaluation criteria regardless of affiliations.

- **Insurance gets a bad rap.** It is something we all need that no one wants to pay for. The wide range of expertise among life insurance agents contributes to the profession's dismal reputation. Regretfully, most insurance agents are trained that every problem can best be solved with an insurance policy. Fortunately, there are many qualified professionals who can add value to your estate- and financial-planning team.

- **Affiliated or independent agent.** Insurance agents are employees of insurance companies, and their loyalty is to that insurance company. Brokers are typically independent and can offer products from several companies, but many agents also can serve as brokers.

What to Look For

Ask for an in-depth analysis of your current insurance policies, not one focusing on reasons to replace existing coverage. The analysis should show how a strategy works in conjunction with estate-planning strategies. Finally, seek out professionals who are happy to share their recommendations with your advisors. Agents reluctant to share information may be recommending something that, although suitable, is not optimal.

Seek Advisors with Overlapping Expertise

Assemble a team of professionals who are familiar with the practices of the other team members. Overlapping expertise protects you from recommendations that, for whatever reason, don't make sense. There can be disagreement between advisors about which strategy or products should be used to accomplish the same goal. This is especially true with investments that will be locked up and illiquid for years, such as insurance, but also applies to private investments, hedge funds, and local real estate.

The tax advantages of insurance contracts make them the playground for creative strategies and complicated structures. Of concern is the long-term nature of implementing any strategy that relies heavily on the tax code not changing. You need to be sure any strategy selected will still be right for you long after the commission has been paid. Having knowledgeable advisors who will not benefit from the decisions is essential.

The Problem: "You Never Call Me"

CPAs are usually considered among the most trustworthy business professionals for good reason. They don't actively market their services, only bill for their time, and are bound by high industry ethical standards. However, these strengths can also be their weakness.

Since most people don't want to receive a call and then get a bill in the mail, CPAs and attorneys have grown reluctant to initiate client contact. As a result, they are frequently brought into the discussion only after important decisions have already been made.

The lack of communication between clients and their CPAs and attorneys is an Achilles' heel. It can lead to frustration when clients lament their own choices and CPAs and attorneys wonder why their clients didn't call prior to making important decisions. The advisor takes the blame, but the client has to live with the outcome. A communication coordinator is needed.

"Mr. Reginald Winthrop, and his attorney, his CPA, and his portfolio manager."

Solution: Identify a Senior Strategic Advisor

1. **Primary point of contact.** Look for one professional to take on the responsibility of being your primary advisor to navigate and integrate myriad issues and options. He or she should be a seasoned, experienced professional who will proactively contact you whenever there is information or actions to be considered.

2. **Facilitator, not bottleneck.** The Senior Strategic Advisor will be your "go-to" advisor for all things family and financial. He or she will be responsible for communication among the family's legal, tax, and insurance advisors.

3. **Breadth and depth of knowledge.** The Senior Strategic Advisor must be knowledgeable across disciplines to be effective in understanding and communicating concepts at a high level and must remain "current" through ongoing continuing education. The Senior Strategic Advisor will participate in important meetings with other advisory team members.

4. **Enhanced communication.** The Senior Strategic Advisor should establish regular communications with the client. The client should expect face-to-face meetings, conference calls, topical updates, event invitations, newsletters, etc. When you find your Senior Strategic Advisor, the rest will be easy.

Summary

1. Advisors sell the best products they have. But the company for which they work and the training they have received can limit them. Differentiate between business practices, experience, and skill sets.

2. Ask for references, work samples, and a scope-of-work estimate prior to engaging. Know what to expect and why.

3. Having a Senior Strategic Advisor to help evaluate and coordinate is key.

NEXT CHAPTER

1. Now that you have a team of qualified advisors and have identified a Senior Strategic Advisor to coordinate communication, the next chapter discusses how to manage your relationship with your new team. Defining the services, quality, cost, and timelines expected will help everyone involved.

2. Establishing clear expectations set in plain language improves your chances of getting great service and everyone working well together.

3. Periodically meet with all your advisors to review what is working well and how the service can improve.

||||||||||

CHAPTER 5

GET GREAT SERVICE FROM YOUR WEALTH ADVISOR

Every new client–advisor relationship requires a leap of faith. The client hopes the new advisor will provide good service, give sound advice, and see the family through good and bad times. The advisor hopes the family will be patient through difficult markets and stay long enough to recoup the sunk cost of onboarding a new relationship. Few clients know how to ensure they receive great service. Establishing proper expectations will help you get the experience you deserve and create the long-lasting, gratifying relationship the advisor seeks.

||||||||

Select a firm with superior service in its DNA.

||||||||

Look for a team with an acute attention to detail. You want your people to define their service as "better than it needs to be." Some companies reward employees for doing as little as possible for the revenue generated. Great advisors, on the other hand, do more than just what is required. Ask them for examples of what they typically do for a client. If it sounds routine, it probably is.

What follows is my idea of exceptional service.

Regular Review Cycles

Formal meetings should occur at least annually and include a financial review and future plans. Cash flow, investment progress, and family dynamics will determine what should be prioritized. A list of common topics follows:

1. **Budgets.** Setting and keeping budgets is a best practice. Reviewing cash-flow needs for living expenses, tax payments, and charitable and investment commitments is essential. Incorporating budgeting into these meetings keeps checkbooks balanced. Very few firms are set up to teach clients how to budget and therefore don't. What gets measured gets managed.

2. **Continuing education.** Staying current on important topics is part of stewardship and sets the example for succeeding generations. However, your advisory team shouldn't swamp you with an endless stream of white papers. The educational materials should be tailored to your interests and aspirations.

1. **Investment policy.** An Investment Policy Statement should be simple, not complex. For most families, two pages should do it. It defines the purpose and time horizon of the money; how much is invested in stocks, bonds, real estate, and cash; how to balance current income and future growth; who is responsible for investment decisions; and how frequently the client and advisors meet. Review this annually.

2. **Relative performance, risk.** Understand what you own and why. Review absolute and relative progress against your goals. Consider absolute returns compared to inflation after taxes and fees. A balanced approach fosters stability and can help preserve purchasing power.

3. **Cumulative results.** Most financial firms focus on reporting time-weighted returns, also referred to as "average annual returns." These measure how the investments performed over a quarter or year and, fair or not, are a proxy for how good or bad your advisor is. I recommend focusing on dollar-weighted results over many years. These cumulative returns are a better measure of how much money you make over time.

4. **Cash flow and year-end tax planning.** For the wealthy, tax planning is critical. April 15th is not Tax Day—every day is Tax Day. Any discussion with your advisors regarding taxes should include anticipated or unusual tax incidents that merit proactive action.

PHILANTHROPY

1. **Family philanthropy.** Whether using a donor-advised fund or foundation, a review of the documentation,

filings, tax returns, and administrative issues ensures proper tax treatment and keeps everyone in the communication loop. Some families capture their values and philosophies in a few sentences reflecting, "Who we are and what we stand for." This can be done in a couple of hours or over a weekend seminar.

2. **Multigenerational involvement.** Informing and educating young adults about why the family gives money to certain causes or institutions can begin as early as the teen years. Over time, the responsibilities of the family philanthropy and finances should shift to adult children. Making grants can be fun and learning investing can be interesting. Learning the administrative aspects is the least interesting, yet a necessary, stage of the journey.

3. **Grant and impact review process.** Learning how to handle requests for money is a valuable life lesson. Instituting a formal grant-request process, or just discussing how to respond, is time well spent. Measuring the impact of past gifts introduces a discipline that has lasting value across a multitude of areas.

4. **Investment reviews.** Learning vocabulary and investment concepts is part of stewardship development. Environmental, Social, and Governance (ESG) and Impact Investing (II) merit understanding. Eventually, the family's role in the community will be up to the next generation.

TAX PLANNING AND COMPLIANCE

1. **Tax law changes, organizational reviews.** Have your tax advisors review legislative updates and court rulings on S-corps, partnerships, pass-through entities, and trusts.

Certain structures are better suited for control, protection, and tax treatment. Refresh regularly.

2. **Entity management.** Ensure all documents of the various legal structures and operating agreements are current and the minutes of meetings are recorded and filed. This meeting is a good time to ensure items such as signatories, electronic passwords, and beneficiary designations are in proper order.

ESTATE PLANNING

1. **Trust checklist.** Families with estate plans that include multiple trusts should have an annual checklist of items to review, which may include notification letters, disbursements, charitable remainder trusts, or loan payments. Maintain a list of these items as well as who is responsible for reviewing them.

2. **Estate planning review.** The composition of the family holdings and structures will drive what should be reviewed and how frequently. In other words, some families have agreements between legal entities, such as loans that need an annual payment or a forgiveness of payment. This is one of the many types of arrangements that require regular reviews. Changes in tax law and family dynamics will drive what new items should be considered. Keep a list of who is responsible for each aspect. Confirm completion of required items.

3. **Tax compliance: state, local, and federal.** Before client-review meetings, your tax advisors should check for tax-law updates or changes that may affect the family. Most changes in tax laws are minor and infrequent.

Regardless, your tax advisor should be tasked with this responsibility as part of the review process.

Risk and Insurance Review

1. **Scope and terms.** Have your property and casualty insurance professional review your exposure and coverage. Ask where gaps exist and avoid overlaps. Checklist:
   A. Property and casualty, umbrella liability
   B. Medical, health, and long-term care
   C. Cyber, information, and online security
   D. Personal: fine art, kidnapping, identity theft, aircraft, offshore, privately owned captive insurance entities for self insurance, etc.

My experience suggests using one insurance carrier can reduce costs and ease the claims process and coverage disputes.

Document Roundup

Maintain a list of important documents and instructions and their locations, including:

- Wills, trusts, tax forms, partnerships, deeds
- Titles, warranties, tax returns
- Healthcare proxies, final instructions
- Marriage, birth, and baptismal certificates and prenuptial agreements
- Military service records
- Crypto assets
- Passwords
- Mobile-phone unlock instructions

Not every family needs every item listed above included in their advisor meetings, but look for an advisory firm that has the right capabilities for you. When you find an advisory firm that is familiar with your issues and how to navigate them, make sure it is set up to give you the quality of service you are seeking. Following the steps above will help ensure you get great service from your wealth advisor.

SUMMARY

1. At the outset of the client–advisor relationship, create a schedule of items to be reviewed together and the frequency of these reviews. Proactively identify areas of interest to seek further education.

2. Involve all constituents, advisors, and family members in these reviews whether they be in person, on video call, or via email. You don't need to rack up hourly expenses, but, periodically, a stitch in time saves nine.

3. Stay up to date. The more complex your finances are, the more frequently you will need to conduct reviews. If you have multiple trusts, LLCs, and other legal entities set up in different states, have one every year.

NEXT CHAPTER

1. Now that you know how to get great service, the next chapter touches on how to be a good client. Appreciating what service providers do for you will ensure they go the extra mile when they can.

2. Have a clear understanding of expectations and what they mean for both of you. Write these expectations out in plain language so you both understand what is to be done.

3. Value what they do for you, and let them do it. Sometimes, you are paying for decades' worth of experience and judgment delivered in minutes.

CHAPTER 6

||||||||||

HOW TO BE A GOOD CLIENT

The adage that the best way to have a good friend is to be a good friend comes to mind. It is a life principle that applies to personal and business relationships alike. In this chapter, I write to remind myself, as well as the reader, that to have good relationships, I need to be the client others want to serve.

There are a few business establishments I go to each week— the coffee shop, the club, and the parking garage—where I am greeted with a warm smile and a hello. The people I encounter in these places are very nice, and I look forward to seeing them. They have learned my preferences, and I, in turn, have learned how to be a good customer.

A key to a mutually satisfying relationship, whether you are a client or a service provider, is a clear understanding of expectations. Whether as a client or customer, once you have found an exceptional service provider, you are well served to know how to keep them.

The following lays out a framework that clients can follow to ensure they receive the experience they desire from their investment advisor.

Relationships Go Both Ways

Trust between client and advisor is paramount. It is obvious the advisor must earn the trust of the client, but clients probably want an advisor who will go the extra mile when needed. Occasionally, this may require the team to stay late, come in early, do deeper research, or make an additional call. Good clients get these services.

Good advisors know that efficient and accurate administrative support is as critical to the client experience as competitive investment results. Both are essential to long-term mutually satisfying relationships. Some firms send mass emails, others require customers to go to a website, and still others require customers to call an eight-hundred number to engage with an automated response system.

Clients want advisors who personalize communications, proactively provide details, and offer to do the work for them. These are the great advisors. However, great advisors only want great clients.

Service Standards: Request It in Writing

My experience is that 70 percent of client satisfaction is derived from smooth and efficient administrative services. The elements of these services vary with the complexity of the family. The scope of services can be as bare bones as sending statements and disbursements or as involved as hosting family meetings.

To ensure strong relationships, the scope of the services should be agreed to in detail at the outset of the engagement. To be a good client, you may need to pin down a talented salesperson and get them to commit to writing what is promised and have the team member responsible for delivering the service concur in writing.

Great advisors want to be sure clients have reasonable expectations when it comes to service and results.

Investment Expectations: Don't Chase Last Year

Disappointment with investment results can be due to either the advisor or the client. Often, it is due to the investor's own behavior. Advisors overpromising results or encouraging unrealistic expectations can also cause friction. Too often, marketers promote investment strategies only after great returns have been experienced. The average person is sold on the result but does not understand how it was achieved nor the probability of it being replicated.

Clients disappointed with the poor short-term results that often follow above-average returns may feel they can do better investing by themselves. In principle, that might be true. However, studies by Dalbar have established that the average investor earns only 50–60 percent of the market returns.[28]

That investor without an advisor contributes to their own eventual disappointment by chasing high returns, seeking rock-bottom fees, or engaging in similarly nonproductive behavior. To be a good client, if the strategy and implementation were sound, don't be disappointed if the short-term results lag. Don't chase past investment results.

"Please compliment Carson on the firewood. He chopped it himself."

---

28 Dana Anspach, "Why Average Investors Earn Below-Average Market Returns," The Balance, last updated April 5, 2021, https://www.thebalancemoney.com/why-average-investors-earn-below-average-market-returns-2388519.

Ten Tips

Common goals of families with wealth include the accumulation, protection, and transfer of assets. To be a good client, find an advisor who will show you why it is hard to become wealthy, why so many families fail to become wealthy, and what you need to do to avoid that common fate.

1. **Select the right advisor in the first place.** Write down your needs and preferences and your reasons for both. List what you liked about your past advisory relationships and what you did not. Know what you want from your advisor and the service experience you expect.

2. **Set high standards.** Seek out the very best provider in each profession. It costs virtually the same to hire a highly qualified advisor as it does to hire a less-qualified one; however, the difference in advice, service, and results can be extraordinary.

3. **Value, not price.** There is a cost to doing high-quality, ethical business. Remember that you are paying for thirty years' worth of experience and judgment, not just thirty minutes of someone's time. When people have trouble differentiating between the breadth, depth, and quality of service of two or more advisors, they regress to price and choose the cheaper option. This may be the advisor's fault, but everyone loses.

4. **Emancipate your advisor from fear.** Many investment advisors feel they might be dumped if their recommendations seem too straightforward or entail too much common sense or if investment activity is too low. Do not encourage your advisor to introduce unnecessary complexity.

5. **Don't haggle about fees for "inactivity."** Some client

portfolios involve very little buying and selling. If they own a great company and their portfolio manager does not buy or sell frequently, some clients wonder why they are paying management fees. It takes more restraint and discipline to do nothing when markets are up or down. After good decisions have been made, most of the time, you should do nothing. If the right strategy is to hold quality assets for decades, let your advisor know you will not fire them for limited trading activity. Studies repeatedly show that high activity lowers investment results.[29]

6. **Avoid second-guessing.** When markets go down, it is easy to point out a strategy that would have worked better. Your advisor should tell you their views and how they impact recommendations. If you agree, live with the consequences. If you disagree, let them know before the poor performance.

7. **Avoid multiple relationships.** If you want an advisor to be thinking about you, have enough assets with them to earn that consideration and let them know they have your complete confidence. If you maintain multiple investment-advisory relationships, you will be pitched higher-risk investments. Avoid setting up a performance "horse race." Eventually, you will be the loser.

8. **Trust, but verify.** I love the old adage, "He uses data like a drunk uses a light post—for support rather than illumination." Ask for data that argues against a recommendation. If your advisor knows both sides well, both of you will be happier.

---

29 Brad M. Barber and Terrance Odean, "Trading Is Hazardous to Your Wealth: The Common Stock Investment Performance of Individual Investors," *The Journal of Finance* 55, no. 2 (April 2000): 773–806, https://doi.org/10.1111/0022-1082.00226.

9. **Be candid and encourage candor.** Few people enjoy confrontation, but if something falls short of your expectations, talk about it, even if it is small. Once a year, ask your advisors how you could be a better client.

10. **Have patience.** Client–advisor relationships are intimate. Only enter into one if you expect it to last for at least years. It may be hard for most people to ignore shiny objects, but things of value take time to unfold.

WRITE IT DOWN

To achieve a lasting mutual understanding, request details in writing. Create a document that answers, "What will my experience be, and what can I expect?" It will help make you a great client and enable your advisory team to be the best they can be.

〰〰〰

"The faintest ink is better than the best memory."
—Chinese proverb

〰〰〰

Summary

1. First, hire the right advisor. Finding a match between your needs and expectations and the advisor's services and skills saves everyone headache and aggravation.

2. Avoid multiple investment relationships. Setting up competition between advisors leads to conflicting advice and more work for you. It can occasionally lead to better outcomes, but not often.

3. Be candid, and expect a few bumps. Even the best-intentioned people will occasionally forget things. Get things in writing, not to protect you legally but to ensure everyone remembers what to do and when.

Next Chapter

1. Now that you have a long-term plan, have assembled a team of advisors, have defined clear expectations, and know how to be a good client, the next chapter will help you "put things in order."

2. Periodically, review your plans to ensure they are up to date. Make sure the right people understand the legal entities, the purpose of each aspect of your plan, and, when the time comes, who is responsible for which items.

3. To have things in good order, take the time to explain why things are as they are.

CHAPTER 7

||||||||||

PUTTING YOUR THINGS IN ORDER

I met with my friend and former boss a few months ago. As we strolled down memory lane, I was reminded of a favorite saying, "The older we get, the better we were."

Twenty-five years prior, he and I introduced a new process to help families write down their hopes and dreams and strategies for how to organize their affairs to achieve their goals. We called the document the "Private Wealth Organizer." The Private Wealth Organizer captured each family's aspirations; contact information; letters to spouses, family, and friends; investment policies; and philanthropic goals. We were also very early in the process of enabling clients to see all their financial accounts on one website.

Part of our initiative was allowing clients to put all their documents online in one secure, safe place. We called it a "digital vault." Today, it is the standard, but in 2001, it was cutting edge.

Private Wealth Organizer

Despite the increasing convenience of everything digital, many people I know like to have a hard copy synopsis of what they have, what it is for, and where it is located. Even today, in 2025, they prefer to have hard copies to read, retain, and refer to. This is not to replace secure electronic records but to make summaries of non-sensitive information accessible.

We recommend clients create a Private Wealth Organizer. It should contain all important family financial, estate, and legal documents. It can also contain letters of instruction, a listing of names and contacts, and important nonlegal items, including letters to loved ones, the histories of family members, and myriad other documents. Each family is unique, so the key idea is to assemble what is important to that person or family.

Words to the "Whys"

When I asked Tom if his spouse fully understood the concepts and intent of their plans, he paused. He wasn't sure. I reminded him that despite regular reviews, most spouses without professional training do not understand all the moving parts when it comes time to implement—meaning, after the first person passes.

To address this common gap, I suggested he make a voice recording or video to explain why each part of the plan had been created and how they all worked together. In other words, explain the "why" behind everything.

The logistics are easy. Sit together, look at the screen, and hit the record button on the video or "voice memo" app on your phone. Then, simply talk through the purpose of each aspect of the plan and how they all work together. As you go through each item, explain in your own words why it was established, what it is supposed to do, and what will happen when one spouse predeceases the other.

"My day? Well, I signed 42 documents in 126 places establishing 17 new legal entities in three jurisdictions. Next week we meet with the attorney and CPA to explain to us why."

CO-CREATE FOR UNDERSTANDING

When the surviving spouse participates in the conversation, the plan makes much more sense to them. I encouraged Tom to have the recording transcribed into a text document and then share it—first with his financial advisor then his attorney.[30] The

---

30 We suggest sending it to your financial advisor, assuming they have knowledge of estate-planning strategies and tactics. Good financial advisors can explain most planning concepts and won't send a bill. Be sure to send it to your attorney for the final review.

advisor could offer straightforward explanations on many items and then send it to the attorney. The attorney would make sure the verbal instructions do not conflict with the will or other documents.

When all of this is done, the couple can review the final document and, if they choose, re-record any information from the final transcript that had been created. After one of them passes, the surviving spouse will have both the written instructions and a recording of their day together. I suspect a few stories and pleasant anecdotes may find their way into the recording.

This shouldn't take a lot of time and is a wonderful gift one spouse can give to the other. It will be appreciated at the time of recording and for many years after. When the time comes, not only has the spouse been fully briefed, but they also have the memory of the day they spent together.

Doing this is an act of love. Time can slip away, so after reading this, stop and schedule a time to do it. No practice needed, and "do overs" are allowed.

Items that could be included in the explanation:

1. Summary of/flow charts for wills, trusts, estate plans
2. Final directives, powers of attorney
3. Deeds, titles, partnerships, agreements
4. Listing of entities
5. Property and casualty coverage and contacts
6. Retirement plans, life insurance
7. Personal financial statements, investment policies
8. Contact lists

Summary

1. Having a written record of goals and the purposes of plans can be liberating.

2. Co-creating, explaining, and re-explaining your plans helps enormously.

3. This act of organization is an act of love.

Next Chapter

1. The next chapter outlines the duties and responsibilities of an Executor of a will.

2. Most people have heard a story where a person dies, and the sorting out of the estate was "a nightmare." Whether the paperwork was incomplete or the family dynamic was strained, the person in charge of overseeing it had a tough job. Learn the dozen small things that should be done *before* the will maker dies.

3. Learn what needs to be done after the deceased has passed and the timing and steps to take to avoid confusion and delays.

CHAPTER 8

HOW TO DIVIDE WITHOUT CONQUERING: GUIDELINES TO AN EXECUTOR

This section is written first and foremost for the person who has to do all the work after a "will maker" dies. Some states refer to this role as the "Personal Representative," and others the "Executor." I will use the term "Executor." Having said that, this applies to anyone who needs to update their estate plan.

It never ceases to amaze me how often I hear people relate the "nightmare" they experienced when a friend or relative died. The difficulty of handling the deceased's personal effects, even when their financial affairs are in good shape, can be overwhelming for most. Fortunately, with a little bit of cooperation and preparation, most of the stickier parts can be avoided.

There are many relatively easy things that should be done before an Executor is called into service. The larger and more complex an estate is, the more care should be taken when planning its disposition. All assets in the deceased's name at the time of death are subject to probate. In addition to the financial and family issues, privacy is paramount to most families, and the will and the disposition of the assets become public record. More importantly, if there are disputes between family members, the proceedings, claims, and counter-claims are all open to the public.[31] It also takes more time and money to settle a probated estate.

The following suggestions are geared to the Executor, who is usually a close family member or the child of the decedent, but most are helpful in all cases. Each state has specific requirements, so be sure to know the ones in yours. A few hours of planning can save a lot of hassle and maybe prevent a lifetime of familial discord.

When You Accept
1. Do What You Can While You Can

When you accept the role of Executor or Co-Executor, there are a handful of things that should be done right away before the will maker dies. This can save both time and trouble.

---

31 Stewart C. W. Weiner, "What's So Horrible About Probate That Makes Everyone Want to Avoid It?," Maddin Hauser, November 27, 2023, https://maddinhauser.com/whats-so-horrible-about-probate-that-makes-everyone-want-to-avoid-it/.

2. Know the Basics

Know the names and contact information of the estate attorney, CPA, investment advisor or financial company, and life-insurance agent.

3. Professional Assistance

At some point, you will want to seek an attorney's assistance. Too many costly mistakes are made by trying to save money on professional services, especially in larger estates.

You can suggest a professional Executor be named in your stead if the estate is complex or there are strained relationships among beneficiaries or family members. It may be better for someone else to be the "bad guy" if there is a difficult message to be delivered. Investing in familial harmony is money well spent.

In lieu of hiring a professional to be the Executor, consider hiring someone with limited authority to carry out specific functions. This is often less expensive, and fees can be better negotiated before the death. Statutory fees for Executors can be higher.

4. Read the Last Will and Testament

Knowing where the will is and what it contains is essential. Some wills contain very sensitive information the will maker does not want revealed until after their death. You don't need to know all the details, but you should know what you are expected to do. Ask the will maker if there are any unusual or specific provisions. If the instructions aren't clear to you, they won't be clear to others. This is also a good time to find out if any of the beneficiaries might be surprised by the provisions of the will. This is not the time to solve family problems, but the Executor should understand the complexities that might arise.

5. Safety Deposit Boxes

Become the co-owner of the safety deposit box, if there is one, so you can get into the box with your own signature. Be certain you have access to a key for the safety deposit box. Do not rely on a "power of attorney"—*it expires upon the principal's passing.*[32] If there is a safe or lock box at the home, make sure you or the attorney knows the combination.

6. Special Bequests and Heirlooms

It is essential for the will maker to have advanced discussions with all relevant people to inform them of his/her intentions. These plans should be written down because people remember things differently. Clarifying the plans while one is alive is better than burying a time bomb that could create lasting problems.

Financial Assets
7. Register Individually Owned Stocks, Savings Bonds

It is rare now, but some people still have investments in the form of paper certificates. Check tax returns and bank accounts for direct deposits to see if dividends have been paid, and move all holdings into a brokerage account. Replacing lost certificates

---

32 "Powers of Attorney," The People's Law Library of Maryland, accessed June 20, 2025, https://www. peoples-law.org/powers-attorney.

is never simple, and it's even more difficult after the owner has died.

8. List of Assets, A.K.A. Personal Financial Statement

Your job will be much easier if there is an updated, comprehensive list of all assets and liabilities, including ownership interests in various legal entities. Ask that the CPA compile one and include account numbers, ownership titles, property, cars, land, employer retirement plans, beneficiary designations, etc. This takes time, but the will maker knows what to look for and where to find it.

9. LLCs, Private Equity, and Direct Investments

Most of the entities' change-in-ownership provisions will be handled according to their bylaws and the estate plan. However, transferring assets owned in the decedent's name and then dividing those interests among beneficiaries can be a long, tedious process. Some partnerships do a good job dealing with estate issues; others do not, particularly if the will maker has interests in partnerships that are part of other partnerships, also known as "feeder funds." Dividing the ownership fairly of something that cannot be sold for several years, and therefore is difficult to value today, is tricky. Try to simplify these issues in advance, if possible.

10. Usernames and Passwords

A significant challenge is to maintain a current inventory of the will maker's usernames and passwords. Computers, phones, emails, bank accounts, and credit cards all require passwords that need to be updated frequently. Consider asking that the will maker's usernames and passwords be categorized into two or three "buckets."

Passwords for non-sensitive accounts can all be the same. Email and very sensitive passwords, such as those for financial accounts, should be different and updated frequently. Ask that this information be kept with the estate attorney, locked in a secure place, or maintained by a digital security company. In the week following the death, begin reviewing everything.

Addressing the complex and changing tax laws is beyond the scope of this chapter. However, it is critical to highlight the benefits that even a few hours of tax planning can have for families and charities.

WHEN THE WILL MAKER DIES
11. DAY ONE

The day the will maker dies, there are three things the Executor must do:

A. Notify the investment advisor and ask him or her to collect and print all the date-of-death valuations.
B. Ask to stop any systematic withdrawals going to banks or other places.
C. Get the keys to the home, and don't let anyone in unless you are there. If there are other beneficiaries, they are expecting you to make sure all the decedent's belongings are present and accounted for. The last thing you want is for one of the beneficiaries to start distributing the deceased's property.

12. Day Two

Notify nursing homes or landlords, and stop subscriptions that will no longer be used. Smaller items, like cable and newspapers, are not time critical, but if you are being charged for a nursing-home unit, move out ASAP. Long-term healthcare insurance will no longer cover it.

A. Ask the funeral home to contact the Social Security Administration to stop future checks. Wait a week, and contact the Social Security Administration to confirm. Automatic deposits completed after death will have to be returned. Request twenty death certificates from the funeral home. This may sound like a lot, but you will need them to transfer financial accounts and real estate holdings as well as for a surprising number of other things. Finally, re-read the will and instructions.

13. Buy a Scanner

Most entities will require original documents, but in situations that do not, they should accept emailed, scanned documents. Having electronic copies of all of your documents, knowing when they were sent and to whom, and confirming receipt can be real time savers.

14. Now, Go Take Care of the Family

At this point, if you have addressed all of the above, you are off to a great start. Go and spend time attending to the emotional needs of the family.

15. REDIRECTING MAIL/CHANGE OF ADDRESS

Redirect the decedent's mail to your address or a post office box to avoid needing to visit the decedent's house every day to collect bills and other mail. This will help in processing claims against the estate and is easily done at the post office or online. When done online (recommended), you have to "prove" you are the person who died. Most use the decedent's still-active credit card to do so. The post office will charge $1.00. Check the box that forwards the mail of "the entire family" to ensure that mail addressed to you, the Executor, is also forwarded.

16. AFTER DEATH CERTIFICATES ARE RECEIVED

Notify all companies sending pension checks—either physical or automatic deposits—and ask them to stop. Every payment sent after death will have to be repaid, and that can be a real hassle. They will request a death certificate. Ask if a copy is sufficient, and if so, be sure to fit the copy on one page, as originals are often oversized.

17. BANK ACCOUNTS

Find the checks and statements for all bank accounts, and notify the bank that the decedent has passed away. If you are not the account's co-owner, the bank will freeze the account immediately. Fortunately, all checks written prior to the date of death will be honored. You will eventually need to set up an "estate of" bank account.

18. Accessing the Safe Deposit Box

If you are not the co-owner of the safe deposit box, you will need to ask the bank about the procedures in your state for obtaining access to it. Generally, you will need certain documentation, such as a death certificate, the will, a marriage certificate, or an Executor appointment, *and* proof you are the spouse, Executor, or descendant for access to be granted. The requirements vary by state, so call the bank before you go to verify what is needed.

19. Which Bank?

Decide if you want to use the decedent's bank or your own. If you want to change banks, it will require two sets of documents, two trips, and an asset transfer. You will need notary services and medallion guarantee stamps (more on this later). For ease, many people just choose to use the decedent's bank.

20. Probate—What to Bring

Each state has specific probate steps, but the first step everywhere is to have the original will, not a copy. Then, you can go online to the state website of the decedent's legal residence and read the specific steps and requirements. Typically, you will need:

- Decedent's Last Will and Testament
- Decedent's full name, address, and social security number
- Death certificate
- Funeral contract or bill
- Estimated value of the estate

- Titles to automobiles
- Full names and addresses of all direct descendants and persons named in the will
- Names and addresses of all the will's witnesses
- Appointment of Resident Agent, if required
- Notice-waiver forms, if applicable
- Your photo ID

21. PROBATE—BEFORE YOU GO

Call ahead. You may need an appointment, and if you live out of state, you may need an in-state (friend or relative) Resident Agent. The Resident Agent form must be signed before you go. There are three types of estates: small, large, and modified (modified means you don't need to file an inventory with the court—which is good). Odds are that yours will be defined as large. Avoid a "full accounting." A full accounting requires cataloging all assets, activities, and independent valuations. It can be costly and time consuming. If there is real estate owned in another state, find out if there are any special requirements regarding it. Finally, decide which bank you will use for the estate checking account ahead of time.

22. AT THE PROBATE COURT

You want the name of the estate to be the decedent's full name, e.g., "Michael Smith Doe," and to use it every time. Also, use your own full name every time you are asked for it. This will avoid confusion or questions regarding initials or middle names.

23. Letters of Testamentary

Get as many Letters of Testamentary as they will give you (ask for at least twelve), and wait for them, even if it takes time, to avoid having to return. Find out how to get more if needed. If given blank forms to fill out at home, get two blank copies for each form in case you make a mistake.

24. Deadlines, Notices, and Bonding

Understand the deadlines for required documents and public notices and the "wait until" dates for forms and filings.

25. After Probate, Before the Bank

You now need to open an "estate of" bank account, but before you do, you need an Entity Identification Number (EIN). Obtaining one takes five minutes online and can be done on your phone (easier on a laptop). Go to www.irs.gov. Choose the option to download the file as a .pdf, and bookmark the page. If you plan to open the account that day, email it to your contact at the bank and call to let them know you are coming over.

26. Old Bank

If you choose to use a bank other than the decedent's for the "estate of" account, notify the old bank right away. Drop off the death certificate and Letters of Testamentary, or let them know they will be mailed (use UPS/FedEx or registered mail) and should arrive soon. It is important to ask for all the accounts in the decedent's name. There may be one or two accounts you don't know about: savings, certificates of deposit, or joint accounts. Get balances and account numbers. With everything paperless these days, be sure to ask so you know all the accounts.

27. Open a Checking Account for the Estate

Set up an estate account and move money into it to pay bills. You will need your Letters of Testamentary, EIN, and death certificate to set up the account. If using the decedent's bank, you will probably be able to write a check from the old account to the new. If changing banks, you may need to write a check from your own account to be refunded later. Familiarize yourself with online access and depositing checks via your mobile phone.

28. Valuations—Attorney–Client Privilege

If a valuation of an asset is required (e.g., private company or partnership interest), have the attorney hire the valuation expert to maintain client–attorney privilege. There is no need to muddy the waters if recent asset transfers have included substantial discounts and might be challenged by the IRS or state tax authority.

29. Real Estate in Another State

If the real property is owned through an LLC or revocable trust, you may be able to avoid this step. However, if the property is owned in the name of the decedent, an ancillary estate will need to be opened. Find a local lawyer because you will need appraisals and a slew of work to be done.

30. Find Everything

Go through the past few years' tax returns and look for dividends, interest, K-1s, partnership payments, and automated deposits. If you do not know where the tax returns are kept, contact the tax preparer for copies. Review email accounts to see if there are any issues that should be addressed, automatic payments that should be stopped, subscriptions that should be cancelled, or people who should be contacted.

31. One-Month Checklist

Notify pensions and retirement plans, subscription vendors, credit cards, the DMV, utilities, and auto and health insurance providers so you can cancel services, accounts, and registrations as appropriate. Contact the life insurance company to claim insurance proceeds, and while you are doing this, change other beneficiary designations and contact the Social Security Administration to process surviving-spouse benefits. Add the deceased's name to the "Deceased Do Not Contact" list maintained by the Data and Marketing Association. Notify club and alumni associations of the death, and send thank you cards to those who sent condolences.

32. Executor Compensation

Being the Executor of an estate takes time, and the person can charge a fee. In many family situations, no fee is charged and only expenses, such as travel, are deducted. However, each state has guidelines as to fair fees.

33. Five Mistakes to Avoid

A. Don't pick and choose from the instructions in the will.
B. Don't keep secrets from the family and beneficiaries.
C. Don't borrow from the estate.
D. Don't be afraid to ask or pay for help when you need it.
E. Pay all debts before distributing proceeds. There can be personal liability if assets are incorrectly distributed, so take your time and do it right.

34. Seek Consensus

Be thoughtful about how to adjust each beneficiary's share of the estate after the heirlooms are distributed. Be sure all involved agree on the economic value of the heirlooms. Perceptions of economic value will vary.

"Fair is not always equal."

What Comes Next?

Eventually, the decedent's tax return will need to be filed as well as a tax return for the estate of the decedent. If you do not already have a tax advisor, or if you feel the complexity of the estate is beyond the scope of your current advisor relationship, seek good tax advice and do what you can as early as you can. The steps that follow the funeral can be tricky, but if done correctly the first time, they need not be overwhelming or frustrating.

Now that the heavy lifting is done, we can proceed to the final step: making sure those who will help oversee the next phase are capable and willing. Navigating family dynamics takes experience, judgment, and compassion. In some cases, it requires the ability to say no. Picking the right people is critical.

Summary

1. Have a conversation with the will maker and review the checklist when you are asked to serve as the Executor or Personal Representative.

2. Inform those who need to be informed, such as legal and tax advisors as well as potential beneficiaries, as appropriate, to avoid misunderstandings.

3. Follow the steps and avoid shortcuts.

NEXT CHAPTER

1. The next chapter explores what it means to be and how to choose a trustee. Being a trustee is a privilege and responsibility. Selecting a person qualified and willing to do the difficult or unpleasant is the crux of the issue.

2. Know what being a trustee entails and select the right combination of talent, capabilities, and compassion.

3. Execute diligently, bring in specialists as needed, and reassess every five years.

CHAPTER 9

||||||||||

IT TAKES MORE THAN TRUST TO BE A GOOD TRUSTEE

A childhood friend of mine had two siblings, one older and one younger. When her grandmother died, it was revealed the grandmother had made my friend the trustee of a trust set up for my friend and her siblings. Sadly, her older sibling had struggled with a substance problem for decades. Over the ensuing years, the responsibility of saying no to repeated requests for extra distributions put an enormous weight on their relationship and led to inevitable discord.

Naming a relative or family friend as trustee sounds like a good idea but can do irreparable harm to relationships. I encourage clients to think long and hard before selecting someone as a trustee just because they are a family member or you trust them. Families who use a thoughtful process to plan their estates should avoid surprises, incorporate contingencies, and select a qualified trustee.

Trustee Selection: Family, Friend, or Financial Institution?

To review the basics, a trust is a legal entity created by the "grantor," a.k.a. the person who contributes the assets to and decides on the terms of the trust. The trustee controls the trust and is empowered to carry out its terms for the benefit of the beneficiaries. There are many types of trusts and hundreds of ways they can be structured. For illustrative purposes, let's assume assets are put in trust for the general benefit of children or grandchildren.

Who should be the family's trustee is among the most important decisions a family must make. The inclination to select a family member or family friend is high.

Family member or friend. When a nonprofessional is named trustee, an assumption is made that they understand the family dynamics and will "do the right thing" if extenuating circumstances arise. A family member or friend acting as trustee may choose not to charge a fee to the trust, so it may be less expensive than hiring a professional. However, the responsibilities of a trustee are extensive, and unless the trustee has reasonable knowledge of the requirements, or commits to learning them, the pitfalls could far outweigh the cost of a professional trustee's fee. Secondly, the ability, capacity, or willingness of the named individual may diminish or the relationship with the family may go sour at some point in the future. It happens, believe me.

Corporate trustee. A corporate trustee is an institution, not a person. The trust department can be named the legal entity responsible for overseeing a trust. Trust departments are knowledgeable about trust laws, restrictions, and requirements, and they should be around for the life of the trust, which may be forty years or more. If they do something wrong, there is a deep pocket to make it right. That is why they charge fees. However, unless your trust assets or banking relationship is large, the service can be impersonal, and the individual administrator often rotates regularly.

Rising and Falling Popularity of Bank Trust Departments

Back in the day, it was common for people to go to the local bank and have the bank create the trust document they would sign to open a trust. When the parents died, the institution managed the trust assets and charged fees for decades. Often, the language of the bank-provided trust document made it nearly impossible for the trust department to be removed as trustee. That created an uninterruptible ongoing revenue stream. Captive clients eventually receive poor service, and that happened frequently with these trusts.

Today, almost all trust documents allow the trust to be moved from one institution to another quite easily. Most documents specify how a trustee can be changed, and trust companies have realized the short-term revenue gains achieved by keeping business against the wishes of the beneficiaries are not worth the reputational damage.

"Yes, I would be happy to discuss increasing the distribution from your trust. How about July? No, not this year. Does the year after work for you?"

FACTORS FOR TRUSTEE SELECTION

- **Complexity, size, and horizon.** Factors guiding trustee selection are the trust's complexity, size, and expected time horizon. If the trust or trusts own significant assets to benefit many generations, subjective assessments will likely be required in the future. For this reason, a professional trustee can be very helpful.

- **If a nonprofessional is chosen,** the first course of action is to have a qualified lawyer explain the terms, requirements, and expectations to the beneficiaries and new trustee. The second is to put a mechanism in place to regularly ensure all that should be done is being done, such as required distributions, waiver letters, tax return filings, and proper documentation of requests, deliberations, and decisions.

Include at the meeting the drafting trust attorney, the trustee, and all adult beneficiaries. The trust attorney should review the terms of the trust and conditions for disbursements and offer general updates of relevant tax laws, if any. This allows the beneficiaries direct access to an informed neutral party and should reinforce the actions and decisions of the trustee, if any are in doubt.

CORPORATE TRUSTEE

If a professional trustee or corporate trust company is selected, the following are a few considerations:

1. **Co-trustees.** If you decide to make a family member, friend, or other nonprofessional a trustee, consider naming a corporate trustee to be a co-trustee. It doesn't save any money, but it helps ensure taxes will be filed on time and any non-standard disbursements will be handled correctly. It also affords the individual trustee "air cover" if discretion is required and requests are denied. This is my clearly favorite option because it takes pressure off the individual trustee to keep abreast of laws, make proper filings, and distribute the right amount of money. It also allows the non-family member to be the "bad cop" who denies requests not allowed in the documents.

2. **Replacing your trustee.** Ensure there are provisions and a process in the trust document to replace the corporate trustee with a qualified successor trustee. This encourages good service. Today, the better trust companies will not accept an assignment without this type of provision.

Because of this, if an unpopular decision is rendered by the corporate trustee, the odds are pretty good it is driven by the law and not motivated by a desire to keep as much money in the trust as possible so their fees will stay higher.

3. **Trust protectors.** Consider specifying a "trust protector." This is usually someone who is empowered to be informed of the activities of the trust and can advise beneficiaries. This can introduce additional expense and complexity but in larger-trust situations is a good option to have.

FINAL THOUGHTS

The financial and emotional costs of an incorrectly administered trust can be very high. Tax penalties, disqualification, or litigation can be expensive and emotionally draining. More importantly, misunderstandings among family members, especially a generation down the line, can be devastating.

As the size, complexity, and time horizon of the trust increase, the importance of proper communication and administration increases exponentially. The selection of the right trustee, whether a friend or professional, is as important as the terms of the trust. Make it wisely.

SUMMARY

1. Know the laws, requirements, and scope of services over the life of the trust before selecting a trustee.

2. Maintain clear communication with the trust beneficiaries, trustee, and trust protector, if there is one.

3. Follow the document, record the proceedings, and keep communication high.

NEXT SECTION

1. The next section discusses how managing wealth is more than managing money; however, good money management counts.

2. Understand the importance of thinking long term, why most investors have historically experienced poor returns, and how to let time and common sense help achieve long-term investing success.

3. Get good help, invest in quality, and don't sweat the small stuff.

PART II

MANAGING
MONEY

"You're Fired"

No, this was not my audition for Donald Trump's 2004 reality television show *The Apprentice*. This was from a client I had worked with for several years and who had experienced above-average performance. To be fair, the client never actually told me he was firing me but that he was transferring his account to a local bank's investment department.

This was the first time in my career I had lost a client. I didn't understand why—a month earlier, we had a meeting and went over his results. They were quite good on an absolute and relative basis. I believed he and his wife left the meeting as pleased as I was, but clearly, that wasn't the case.

He was kind enough to tell me why they decided to transfer. It was because, despite his good performance, in his mind (and therefore, in reality), he was exposed to too much risk. I had him invested in a few mutual funds, one of which was a fund with stocks and bonds. The performance was very good, and he equated that with risk. When I explained why his risk was less than it seemed, I simply proved I was not listening. Since then, I have lost a few clients but not many and none because I wasn't listening.

In Part III, I will go over the "Art of Listening." In this section, I show that the lesson when managing money is *success is not just a comparison to a popular index*. Success in managing money is achieving peace of mind.

Managing Money

Managing wealth is more than managing money, but the thoughtful management of assets is essential.

In Part II, I highlight some of the reasons why the average person does not manage their money well. I touch on the behavioral instincts and societal pressures that make managing your own money so difficult. Accumulating money is not the goal; achieving happiness and peace of mind is. Our ability to ignore the media noise and shiny objects and defer gratification plays a key part.

Whether you manage your own money or hire advisors, adopt a framework to help create a steady stream of rising income. If your income increases at a rate in excess of inflation after taxes and expenses, your standard of living should improve. That should help you attain financial independence on the road to peace of mind.

Next, I talk about what to do if you suddenly find yourself in the position of being responsible for managing a lot of money. A key theme is to take your time and don't take on a lot of risk to get "richer." My investing philosophy is geared toward helping to create diverse, secure streams of rising income and why I believe dividends still matter.

Families of affluence have younger family members who need to learn how to be financially independent. For younger people who wonder if they can attain financial independence, I offer the simple process of dollar cost averaging. I touch on the universal truism of avoiding making aggressive bets, which rarely work out. Paraphrasing Nancy Reagan, just say no.

The final chapter in this section is on portfolio management. Most people are well served by earning the market averages, and frankly, that should be the goal. History has shown it is very hard for most people to successfully manage their own portfolios, even when simply "average" is the goal.

Earning "above average" investment returns takes an unusual mindset—a mindset where you must be comfortable being alone in your point of view, be willing to do more than cursory research, and be able to challenge yourself about why your ideas may be wrong. Less than 15 percent of investors can achieve consistent "above average" results.[33] I examine what it takes and why it is so hard to do.

33   Druckenmiller, "DealBook Conference 2015—The Other Investors' Perspective," https://www.youtube. com/watch?v=loYjPekmccs.

CHAPTER 10

IF MANAGING MONEY IS SO EASY, WHY AREN'T MORE PEOPLE RICH?

When I began my career in financial services, I was introduced to a new investment strategy or fad every other year. Each seemed better than the last. I learned to buy "stocks at a discount to book value" then "growth stocks with momentum." The next trend was to "diversify into international stocks" followed by "rotating and rebalancing" as styles went in and out of favor.

Along the way, I realized most investors don't make a lot of money, and certainly not after paying taxes and fees. It occurred to me that I needed to first understand *why people did not do well* investing in order to avoid those mistakes.

I believe we face a societal problem due to the unrelenting encouragement to spend money. Glamorizing living beyond one's means often leads to dissatisfaction. A few years ago, a study found 40 percent of Americans were one paycheck away from poverty.[34] More recently, the number of Americans considering filing for bankruptcy is the highest it's been since the COVID-19 pandemic.[35]

Over the long term, the savings of a typical family do not grow as much as they should with better guidance.[36] As a result of poor planning and investing, another survey found that 64 percent of Americans will retire "broke."[37]

A good start to achieving better outcomes is knowing how to avoid a few unforced errors.

WHY AREN'T MORE PEOPLE RICH?

I see many culprits as to why people are not rich: low savings, high consumption, taxes, inflation. A lesser understood culprit, however, is poor investing. Even among those who had a sizable amount of money decades earlier, most couldn't hold onto it. Let me explain.

---

34 Aimee Picchi, "40% of Americans Only One Missed Paycheck Away from Poverty," CBS News, January 19, 2019, https://www.cbsnews.com/news/40-of-americans-one-step-from-poverty-if-they-miss-a-paycheck/.

35 Daniel Miller, "Americans Considering Filing for Bankruptcy Hits Highest Level Since Pandemic," Fox 35 Orlando, April 18, 2025, https://www.fox35orlando.com/news/americans-consider-filing-bankruptcy-high-level.

36 Emmie Martin, "65% of Americans Save Little or Nothing—and Half Could End Up Struggling in Retirement," CNBC, last updated June 16, 2020, https://www.cnbc.com/2018/03/15/bankrate-65-percent-of-americans-save-little-or-nothing.html.

37 Sean Dennison, "64% of Americans Aren't Prepared for Retirement—and 48% Don't Care," GOBankingRates, September 23, 2019, https://www.gobankingrates.com/retirement/planning/why-americans-will-retire-broke/.

If you had $1 million invested passively in the S&P 500 equivalent in 1935,[38] with no withdrawals and no taxes, it would have grown to about $12.6 billion at the end of 2024.[39] A million dollars was a lot of money in 1935, but records indicate that even during the Great Depression, there were between five and ten thousand millionaire families in the US.[40] Since we are ignoring taxes, let's just say five thousand to keep it simple.

WHERE DID IT ALL GO?

If each of the five thousand families had two children, there would be twelve families (assuming four people per family) today for each one living in 1935. That means if there were five thousand millionaire families in 1935, they would have spawned sixty thousand billionaire families four generations later(actually $12 billion families, but who's counting). That is to say sixty thousand billionaire families should exist today if their investment results had been able to match the returns of a passive investment in the US stock market. Let's take a closer look.

According to *Forbes*, there are about nine hundred billionaire families in the US, and virtually none of them derived their money from their ancestors living in 1935.[41] What happened to the other 98.5 percent? Was it so hard to match the returns of a passive investment in the US stock market? Evidently, it was.

---

38   The Standard & Poor's 500 index was not created until 1957, so we use the Dow Jones Industrial Average as a proxy.

39   PK, "S&P 500 Return Calculator, with Dividend Reinvestment," DQYDJ, accessed June 20, 2025, https://dqydj.com/sp-500-return-calculator/.

40   Kevin Phillips, *The Politics of Rich and Poor: Wealth and the American Electorate in the Reagan Aftermath* (New York: l), Random House (1990), 239.

41   Chase Peterson-Withorn et al., eds., "World's Billionaires List: The Richest in 2025," *Forbes*, accessed June 20, 2025, https://www.forbes.com/billionaires/.

What Makes Getting the "Index" Return So Difficult?

Besides consumption and taxes, two major investment-related enemies inhibit the successful growth of savings. We all know the financial industry takes a toll through fees, commissions, and spreads. That takes a large fraction of potential earnings. However, the second, and even bigger, problem is ourselves.

〰〰〰

It turns out, it is incredibly challenging for do-it-yourself individuals to capture even the passive returns offered by the market.

〰〰〰

The reality is that when it comes to investing, we are our own worst enemy. Extensive research shows that humans carry enormous baggage from our evolutionary past. That baggage, as it turns out, is a hindrance to success in the twenty-first century financial environment.[42]

Good Then, Bad Now?

Our instincts may have saved us from being eaten by predators and wild animals thousands of years ago, but today, they make us sitting ducks. One well known study by Barber and Odean titled "Trading Is Hazardous to Your Wealth" analyzed over sixty thousand households of active, nonprofessional investors.[43] They found that on average, these active traders lost 6

---

42 Daniel Kahneman, *Thinking Fast and Slow* (New York: Farrar, Straus and Giroux, 2011), 20.

43 Barber and Odean, "Trading Is Hazardous to Your Wealth: The Common Stock Investment Performance of Individual Investors."

percent per year in the stock market. This occurred because people react emotionally to short-term stimuli and generally buy high and sell low. Wow!

What can we do to prevent ourselves from being fleeced or fleecing ourselves? It turns out there has been a potential solution available for more than sixty years known as Modern Portfolio Theory. This concept was invented by Harry Markowitz, who won the Nobel Prize for his paper "Portfolio Selection," and enabled John Bogle to kickstart the $16 trillion passive investment industry.[44] The "passive investment industry" comprises hundreds of low-cost mutual funds and ETFs that mimic popular indexes, most notably Standard & Poor's (S&P) 500 index.

The largest and most widely known index funds are the Vanguard S&P 500 fund, State Street's SPY ETF, and Blackrock's iShare Core S&P 500 fund.

The idea behind Modern Portfolio Theory is to seek efficient diversification by investing across an entire market. There is only one problem: most people can't accept this approach. And even those who try generally don't stick with it.[45]

---

44   Harry Markowitz, "Portfolio Selection," *The Journal of Finance* 7, no. 1 (March 1952): 77–91, https://doi.org/10.2307/2975974; Investment Company Institute, "Active and Index Combined Long-Term Mutual Funds and Exchange-Traded Funds (ETFs): April 2025," press release, accessed June 20, 2025, https://www.ici.org/research/stats/combined_active_index.

45   Lawrence S. Pratt, "Why Most Investors Fail," American Institute for Economic Research, accessed June 20, 2025, https://aier.org/why-most-investors-fail/.

Cognitive Bias at Work Again

Part of the problem is we don't like to see ourselves as passive. It goes against our human nature because we like to feel in control and proactive.[46] As investors, our bias toward action hurts us.

Secondly, stock market bubbles do occasionally occur.[47] The tyranny of passive index investing—and this is a real problem—is that not only does it prevent us from avoiding investing in bubbles, but passive investing also has the perverse tendency to make us invest more heavily in the most expensive stocks at the height of valuations.

Passive Isn't Perfect

To illustrate this point, take the Japanese stock market bubble in 1989. Those who mindlessly allocated assets to a global equity index paid a price. An example of how "everything Japan" was so expensive in 1989: it was purported that the one square mile under the Imperial Palace in Tokyo was worth more than all of California. At that time, a passively managed, capital-weighted portfolio would have been 43 percent invested in Japanese equities. Then, the price of Japanese equities collapsed. It took thirty-two years for Japanese equities to recover enough to surpass their 1989 peak, which they finally did in 2021.[48]

---

46   Lauren A. Leotti et al., "Born to Choose: The Origins and Value of the Need for Control," *Trends in Cognitive Sciences* 14, no. 10 (October 2010): 457–463, https://doi.org/10.1016/j.tics.2010.08.001.

47   Ramsey Shaffer, "The Top 10 Biggest Asset Bubbles of All-Time," *Uptrends* (blog), August 17, 2024, https://www.uptrends.ai/article/the-top-10-biggest-asset-bubbles-of-all-time.

48   "Japan: The Ultimate Stock Market Crash," DIY Investor, March 9, 2025, https://www.diyinvestor.net/japan-the-ultimate-stock-market-crash/.

Is 35 Percent of a Good Thing Too Much?

At times throughout history, the most popular index and related passive funds have experienced nearly a 40 percent concentration in industries-related companies. In 2024, the concentration was severe, dominated by five companies that accounted for over 28 percent of the broad-index and passive index funds.[49] The risk of repeating the mistakes of the past are high indeed.

At the end of 2024, a similar trend emerged when passive index funds enjoyed record inflows, surpassing the previous record set in 2021.[50] Perhaps not surprising was the dramatic market sell-off that followed in 2022. Only time will tell, but an argument can be made that the 35 percent-plus of the value of the S&P 500 index comprising seven companies in December of 2024 will lead to another dramatic sell-off or just lackluster returns in the subsequent few years. This concentration of the "Magnificent Seven," dominated by one advanced microchip manufacturer, Nvidia, may be similar to the fate of Cisco twenty-five years earlier. Cisco peaked in 2000, and at the end of 2024, Cisco's price remained lower than its price in 2000.[51]

49 Muslim Farooque, "Tech Titans Take Over: S&P 500's Top 5 Companies Hit Record 28.8% Weight," GuruFocus, January 8, 2025, https://www.gurufocus.com/news/2650350/tech-titans-take-over-sp-500s-top-5-companies-hit-record-288-weight.

50 Ryan Jackson, "ETF Flows Punctuate Record Year in December," Funds, Morningstar, January 6, 2025, https://www.morningstar.com/funds/etf-flows-punctuate-record-year-december.

51 Paul Hodges, "Stock Market Bubbles Follow the Same Pattern, as Nvidia and Cisco Confirm," Chemicals and the Economy (blog), Independent Commodity Intelligence Services, June 23, 2024, https://www.icis.com/chemicals-and-the-economy/2024/06/stock-market-bubbles-follow-the-same-pattern-as-nvidia-and-cisco-confirm/.

"Inactive Investing": A Better Solution

In my opinion, a solution is needed that both resonates with people and keeps them safe from their worst instincts. An investment approach is needed that keeps us invested; it must be understandable and sufficiently diversified. A new way of investing is needed that combines the benefits of passive investing with what is good in active investing.

What if you could combine Warren Buffett's value investing approach with Charlie Munger's common sense? In other words, be thoughtful about what you own, own only high-quality companies, hold onto them for a long time, and only sell when the industry outlook or the management deteriorates materially.

No one set of rules can capture all the Buffett/Munger genius. Yet, if you could thoughtfully and systematically invest in an easy-to-understand manner, I believe you would be more likely to stay the course. The goal is to avoid chasing markets, buying "high," and later selling in despondence near market bottoms. What if we could combine a few simple principles and common sense?

Not Passive, but Not Active

"Inactive" investing means giving thought to what you want to own, buying stock in those companies, and then letting the company's management, employees, and customers deliver the dividends and compounding returns. This kind of "passive" investing, in other words buying a fund mimicking the S&P 500 index, suggests that you accept what someone else (the index composition committee at the company receiving royalty payments from the use of the brand) decides without thought.

Passive index investing started out as a low-cost, easy-to-understand method of long-term investing to help build wealth accumulation. However, for most, human behavior got in the way.

Virtually every financial services provider has programs that recommend a simple solution to a complex problem. Whether it be a robo-advisor or global investment committee, the easier it is to start, the easier it is to abandon.

The key to investing success is not the brand name nor easy-to-use mobile app. In my opinion, the key is finding someone who can help you start an intelligent plan and stick with it. Someone who can help you get it done—correctly. Few have the training to know what to do. Even fewer have the patience required to stay with a good program when a crisis hits.

"How did we get so rich? The old-fashioned way, of course. We inherited it."

Very Hard to Stay "Above Average"

The reason more people aren't rich is because, definitionally, the majority of us are truly average. We do what others do, follow what we see, and are genetically predisposed to be average. To become wealthy, one must be able to do things others are unable or unwilling to do and do them for long periods of time with patience and persistence. Alternatively, one must be wise enough to seek out and discern superior advice *and then take it.*

Summary

1. Though it may not be easy to get and stay rich, it is more than possible to gain financial independence. Most rich people do not stay rich.

2. Survival instincts and our human nature can work against being a good investor.

3. Active trading leads to losses. My recommendation is to adopt the proper mindset, have an investment philosophy, and implement a thoughtful plan you don't tinker with too much.

Next Chapter

1. The next chapter contemplates investment philosophy. In life and when investing, it's a good idea to know how and why you are making decisions before you start. Think deeply about how to invest before you do.

2. Seek enough wealth to be financially independent. As long as you stick to your plan, this should help you achieve peace of mind. Avoid speculating on fads and risky ventures. Patience, conservatism, and inactivity are not bad things.

3. Diversification to a point is good. Always have some cash: not too much, not too little.

CHAPTER 11

|||||||||||

DEVELOP YOUR INVESTMENT PHILOSOPHY

Like most financial advisors, I didn't grow up with money. My parents taught me about "saving," but that was it. When I was in college, a fraternity brother explained to me how he was buying "options" on stocks and how he could make a fortune while sitting in class. I was fascinated but didn't have enough money to open an account and try. As it turned out, I was lucky. My friend didn't sit in too many classes and lost the money his parents gave him for tuition. When his parents showed up for his graduation a couple years later, he was nowhere to be found. Sad but true story. (Note to self: *pick a better peer group next time you attend college.*)

When I entered the investment field shortly after graduation, financial advisors were called "account executives" and taught one thing: "more was better." Over time, the mantra changed.

"More" was still better, but attaining the "highest risk-adjusted return" was best. This is an important point that I will cover later.

Today, most advisors are trained to teach their clients that seeking the highest risk-adjusted returns is how money should be managed. This has merit in the classroom, academia, and committee-run organizations where the person in charge can be fired for short-term performance disappointments. In the real world of managing long-term, tax-sensitive family money, it misses the point.

||||||||

The real goal for regular people is to have sufficient cash flow that increases at a rate to steadily improve one's purchasing power.

||||||||

It's for this reason I encourage clients managing their own or family money to develop an investment philosophy. This establishes a framework for how you think about financial assets, their purpose, and the role they play. Whether you plan to manage your funds yourself or hire advisors, the first essential step is to write down what you want to accomplish. Writing down a sound investment philosophy that will stand the test of time can determine the difference between good and bad outcomes.

KNOW WHY YOU ARE INVESTING

In my opinion, investors should be in the business of accumulating profits and dividends. Speculating whether the market is going to go up or down is a loser's game. The largest drag on wealth accumulation is poor decisions by investors. Poor investment decisions are usually the result of (1) the lack of a sound investment strategy and (2) the inability to stick to a sound strategy during times of exuberance and despair.

TIME AND ASSET ALLOCATION

Being around wealthy families taught me to allocate assets first by time horizon then by income, risk, and return potential. Time segments:

1. Liquidity—Enough cash for a year or two
2. Legacy—What you plan to leave to your heirs
3. Lifestyle income—Everything in between

"Begin today to reap benefits tomorrow."

This mindset can be especially helpful for families with aging patriarchs and matriarchs to maintain a healthy chunk of "won't ever need" funds in long-term, potentially illiquid assets. The legacy segment can be real estate, operating businesses, intellectual property, royalties, or holding companies.

How Many Asset Classes

Think about diversification in four asset classes: real estate, stocks, bonds, and cash.

- Real estate—Preferably local and cash positive
- Cash and short bonds—One to three years' worth of living expenses
- Stocks—Financially strong, dividend paying

What Do You Want to Own?

Over the last forty years, investment professionals have taught us to invest in "styles"—value, growth, large, small, international, emerging markets, and others. I was there near the beginning and know all the academic studies and arguments for this approach.

However, whether you buy a passive index fund, build a portfolio for yourself, or outsource it, I suggest you set aside the concept "styles" and start with the basics. If you owned a business, what characteristics would you want your company to have?

Consider seeking businesses or investments with:

- Lower debt, strong free cash flow
- A history of reinvesting capital at higher-than-average rates of return
- Consistent earnings, generally growing

If you were able to assemble a portfolio like this and the companies continued to do well, there should be few reasons you would want to sell them. Companies that can be held for a long time are ideal, but no human endeavor can remain "above average" forever.

DIVERSIFICATION FOR TAXABLE INVESTORS

We have been taught that diversification reduces "risk" and increases "returns." As discussed in the prior chapter, this was first introduced by Harry Markowitz in the 1950s and has been popularized as Modern Portfolio Theory. Over the ensuing roughly seventy-five years, many of the nuances of the original paper, the context and conclusions, have been lost. Most financial professionals are not aware of the limitations Markowitz described in the opening paragraphs of "Portfolio Selection."[52] The wealth-management industry (compliance, research, advisor training, sales materials, recommendations, and client reporting) relies on the assumptions that more diversification is better and "rebalancing," the regular selling of assets that have

---

52 In Markowitz's paper "Portfolio Selection," the first sentence establishes that we enter into this process with experiences, expectations, and biases that affect how we think about the math of portfolio management: "The process of selecting a portfolio may be divided into two stages. The first stage starts with observation and experience and ends with beliefs about the future performances of available securities. The second stage starts with the relevant beliefs about future performances and ends with the choice of portfolio. This paper is concerned with the second stage." He acknowledges that our individual beliefs affect the outcome and chooses to defer that and focus on the calculations; Markowitz, "Portfolio Selection," 77.

appreciated to be reinvested in assets that have not, reduces portfolio volatility and is therefore "safer."

When Does Diversification Cause Diworsification?

Both of these assumptions are true, up to a point. For example, owning two stocks is "safer" than owning one. Owning ten stocks is safer than owning two. Owning twenty-five stocks is safer than owning ten. At some point, one should ask, "How much safer do I need to be? Is owning a thousand stocks safer than owning twenty-five?" Statistically, yes, but the incremental safety offered by many additional stocks may be insignificant. The question that should be asked at the same time is whether the fiftieth stock added to the portfolio has as high a return potential as your top five.

"He uses statistics like a drunk uses a lamp post - for support rather than illumination."

A second industry "truth" is that rebalancing is "safer." What is less clear is when to rebalance, how much to rebalance, and into which asset to rebalance. What is uniformly ignored is whether or not taxes are due when capital gains are realized.

In retirement plans, where there are no taxes due on gains, rebalancing makes more sense, but that still does not address when to sell which asset that appreciated and into which assets the proceeds should go.

THE TAX MAN COMETH

These two topics—diversification and rebalancing—are extremely important when investing taxable assets but ignore the negative effect of taxes on capital gains. The investment industry is prohibited from giving tax advice, so it is silent on the tax issue. In the real world, taxes matter because they reduce the amount available for compounding.

You will notice the richest people in the world only selectively follow the advice of diversification and typically own their largest assets for years if not decades.[53] I will generalize by saying owning more than twenty-five stocks in a portfolio probably does not reduce risk meaningfully. As to rebalancing, when managing taxable portfolios, be slow to buy and, when you have made a good decision, even slower to sell.

How much to diversify and into which assets is an art, not a

---

53 Shankar Parameshwaran, "How the Wealthiest Got to Where They Are," *Knowledge at Wharton*, Wharton School of the University of Pennsylvania, March 7, 2023, https://knowledge.wharton.upenn. edu/article/how-the-wealthiest-got-to-where-they-are/.

science. Avoid people and programs that make it seem simple or obvious. It is neither.

Do-It-Yourself or Outsource?

Most people with modest assets should probably simply buy a couple of low-cost index funds. People with significant assets are well advised to enlist professional assistance. The modest incremental cost of wise advice is worth the benefits of service, customization, and tailored advice many times over.

Regardless, all investors should know how they want their money managed—whether they make the decisions themselves or outsource them. This will help you select the right advisor *and* should help you withstand the urge to change strategies at the wrong time.

How Much Cash?

Throughout this book, I mention the benefits of holding some cash. If you have little or no debt and reliable positive cash flow from a job, business, or properties, the amount should be modest. However, there should always be some.

> *"People rarely think about the value of having cash on hand until they try to borrow it from someone."*
> —*Warren Buffett*

The following story is from my childhood, when I was eight or ten years old. It sheds light on how I think about life, money, and opportunity and is a lesson about the benefits of financial security—and how to get and stay financially secure.

"Did We Get the Loan?"

Growing up, my family always took a one-week vacation during the first week in June (the rental rates went up the second week). My parents and their six kids "luxuriated" in a non-air-conditioned, no-television, two-bedroom-and-a-pull-out-couch rental on the beach. You can correctly surmise we were not "rolling in it."

These weeks were always great, but one year, my dad was pre-occupied. In between riding waves and tossing the football, he kept sneaking back to use the pay phone to call long distance. He called so often he must have spent ten dollars in dimes!

On the third day, he finally got the news for which he had been praying. Poch Hardware got the Small Business Loan that would keep the store afloat. Because he was able to get cash when he desperately needed it, the family business survived. I didn't realize it at the time, but had he not gotten that loan, our lives would have been very different.

There have been times when I didn't have enough cash to meet an obligation. It took me a couple of times before I took that lesson to heart and never let it happen again. If you are lucky, you learn that lesson early in life. The importance of having cash when you really, really need it can be inestimable.

Summary

1. It is hard to go wrong investing in quality. Ignore fads and avoid leverage.

2. Don't over diversify, and keep things as simple as possible.

3. When you need it, few things are more important than having cash.

Next Chapter

1. The next chapter delves into investment strategy. Greg Norman, the famous PGA golf champion, used to describe a great approach shot to the green as, "Happiness is a long walk with a putter." In investing terms, I believe happiness is a diverse stream of income reliably rising at a rate in excess of inflation after taxes and expenses.

2. Companies with increasing dividends have impressive long-term total returns.[54]

3. Selecting the right companies at the right prices and then not selling after a big gain is harder than it sounds.

---

54 Spencer Jakab, "Why Investors Are Right to Love Dividends," *The Wall Street Journal*, June 30, 2025, https://www.wsj.com/finance/investing/dividend-investing-stocks-volatility-068c4e5a?st=21Ttp4.

CHAPTER 12

INVESTING FOR FUTURE CASH FLOW

Portfolios focused on growing dividends may deliver strong long-term returns regardless of the market cycle. Dividend-paying companies, in general, tend to be higher quality and historically have had stronger balance sheets than non-dividend-paying companies. There have always been exceptions, such as Berkshire Hathaway and, in the last few years, a few technology companies. However, companies that consistently pay dividends demonstrate financial stability.[55] To me, that means safer. There are many ways to approach investing in equities. For those who want to earn competitive returns with less volatility and anxiety, owning companies that pay steady and rising incomes may make sense. Regardless of the current environment, the importance of dividends and their contribu-

---

55 Stephan A. Abraham, "Is Dividend Investing a Good Strategy?," Investopedia, last updated December 2, 2024, https://www.investopedia.com/articles/basics/11/due-dilligence-on-dividends.asp.

tion to overall total return, for new and experienced investors alike, should not be overlooked.

||||||||

"The true investor...will do better if he forgets about the stock market and pays attention to his dividend returns and to the operating results of his companies."
—Benjamin Graham, The Intelligent Investor: A Book of Practical Counsel

||||||||

DIVIDENDS ACCOUNT FOR 30–40% + OF TOTAL RETURN

History is replete with extended periods of time when growth-oriented stocks outperformed income-oriented stocks. The Nifty Fifty in the 1960s and 1970s was a group of fifty stocks thought to have almost unlimited growth potential.[56] As a result, their stock prices became ridiculously highly valued and subsequently fell precipitously. The internet boom and dot-com run-up of the 1990s was a similar time, when many assumed the profitability of internet-based companies would go up forever. More recently, five companies—Facebook, Apple, Amazon, Netflix, and Google (a.k.a. the FAANG)—and the "Magnificent Seven"[57] in the 2020s are testing a similar assumption: high growth for a long time is highly certain.

---

56 James Chen, "Nifty Fifty: What It Is and How It Works," Investopedia, last updated August 17, 2024, https://www.investopedia.com/terms/n/niftyfifty.asp.

57 Cedric Thompson, "Magnificent 7 Stocks: What You Need to Know," Investopedia, last updated May 27, 2025, https://www.investopedia.com/magnificent-seven-stocks-8402262.

For those with prescient vision who can say when these trends will shift, please call me. For the rest of us—those who wish to help achieve steadily rising cash flow—consider having dividend-paying stocks as a core part of your long-term portfolio.

Dividend stocks, as a group, have experienced less volatility year to year, and they have outperformed non-dividend-paying stocks as well.[58] During bull markets, investors often forget that total return comes from two sources: dividends and price appreciation. In fact, over the last ninety-plus years, dividends have accounted for roughly 40 percent of the total return equation.[59]

Dividends have been a significant component of total return

S&P 500 Index returns from dividends and capital appreciation

■ Dividends   ■ Capital appreciation   ■ Capital depreciation

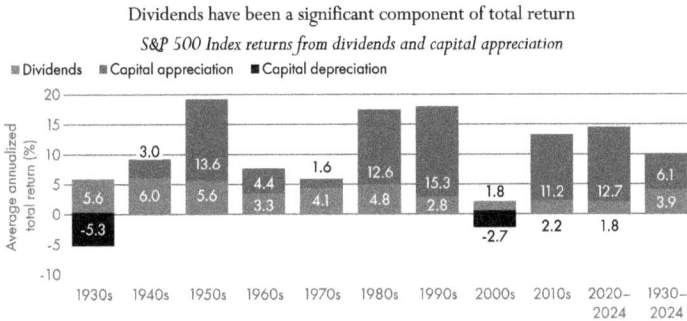

	1930s	1940s	1950s	1960s	1970s	1980s	1990s	2000s	2010s	2020–2024	1930–2024
Capital appreciation		3.0	13.6		1.6	12.6	15.3		11.2	12.7	6.1
Dividends	5.6	6.0	5.6	4.4	4.1	4.8	2.8	1.8	2.2	1.8	3.9
				3.3							
Capital depreciation	-5.3							-2.7			

Ned Davis Research, Inc., December, 2024

Investors who focus solely on price appreciation are implicitly pegging their total return only to the price change of the stocks they own. However, as history reveals, this can lead to disappointing results for investors over long timeframes. With equity

---

58   Jeremy J. Siegel, *The Future for Investors: Why the Tried and the True Triumph over the Bold and the New* (Westminster: Crown Currency, 2005), 126.

59   David Park and David A. Chalupnik, *Why Dividend Growth?* (Nuveen, February 2025), 1, https://documents. nuveen.com/Documents/Global/Default.aspx?uniqueId=5d8a964c-cbcf-4a07-b181-eb6ace0eb3b4; "The Power of Dividends: Past, Present, and Future," (blog) Hartford Funds, accessed June 20, 2025, https://www. hartfordfunds.com/insights/market-perspectives/equity/the-power-of-dividends.html.

prices hovering near all-time highs at the end of 2024, investors could be disappointed with price returns over the next ten years.

At my firm, we believe a better approach may be to own companies that focus on growing their cash flows, increasing dividends, and repurchasing shares.

INCREASING DIVIDEND-PAYING STOCKS OUTPERFORM

There have been many studies over the years that lead to the same conclusion: owning stock that regularly increases its dividends earns attractive returns. Over time, dividend-paying stocks, and in particular the companies able to grow their dividends, outperform non-dividend-paying companies.[60]

Returns of S&P 500 Index stocks by dividend policy: Growth of $100 (1973–2024)

$15,874 Dividend growers and initiators

$9,697 Dividend payers

$4,618 Equal-weighted S&P 500 Index

$2,983 No change in dividend policy

$899 Dividend nonpayers

$63 Dividend cutters and eliminators

---

60 For example, Johnson & Johnson has increased its dividend for more than sixty years. In 1990, split adjusted, it paid an annual dividend of $0.07 per share. In 2000, it grew to $0.32 per share. In 2010, it was $1.35, and in 2020, it was $3.45. Recently, in early 2025, it was $4.85. In addition to the increasing cash dividend, during this thirty-five-year period, the share prices grew from $3.41 to $165. Most would consider this a very attractive return; "The Power of Dividends: Past, Present, and Future," https://www.hartfordfunds.com/insights/market-perspectives/equity/the-power-of-dividends.html.

Study after study concludes the same thing. Whether after a bull market or a bear market, whether after growth stocks do well or poorly, as long as the time period includes a full market cycle, companies that pay and grow their dividends tend to outperform other companies.

For example, in a 2018 study by Ken French, which looked at the period between 1928 and 2017, dividend-paying stocks significantly outperformed the S&P 500 index.

This will be cyclical, and when non-dividend-paying stocks (like high-growth technology) outperform for a few years, such as during the dot-com run-up of the late 1990s and recently from 2020 through 2024, it is usually a very good time to own the companies that reliably grow their dividends.

COMPOUND ANNUAL GROWTH RATE (%) FOR US STOCKS BY DIVIDEND YIELD QUINTILE BY DECADE (1930–2024)

	S&P 500 INDEX	1ST QUINTILE	2ND QUINTILE	3RD QUINTILE	4TH QUINTILE	5TH QUINTILE
Jan 1930 to Dec 1939	−0.20	−2.36	0.61	−2.34	−0.38	2.07
Jan 1940 to Dec 1949	9.51	13.92	13.06	10.26	8.63	6.83
Jan 1950 to Dec 1959	18.33	18.52	20.31	18.47	16.57	19.81
Jan 1960 to Dec 1969	8.26	8.82	8.90	6.46	7.97	9.30
Jan 1970 to Dec 1979	6.05	9.67	10.22	7.00	7.57	3.94
Jan 1980 to Dec 1989	16.80	20.23	19.62	17.20	16.19	14.65
Jan 1990 to Dec 1999	17.96	12.37	15.54	15.06	18.10	18.93
Jan 2000 to Dec 2009	−0.44	5.57	4.15	4.21	1.99	−1.75
Jan 2010 to Dec 2019	13.65	12.98	13.25	14.15	13.68	10.85
Jan 2020 to Dec 2024	14.16	12.04	10.34	9.29	16.62	20.19

As of 12/31/24. Past performance does not guarantee future results. Indices are unmanaged and not available for direct investment. US stocks are represented by the S&P 500 Index. Chart represents the compound annual growth rate (%) for US stocks by dividend yield quintile by decade from 1930-2019 and January 2020-December 2024. For illustrative purposes only. Data Sources: Wellington Management and Hartford Funds, 3/25.

Increasing Dividends and Yield on Cost

I believe a key benefit to long-term investors who buy and hold high-quality dividend stocks is rising cash flow. Given enough time, the annual dividend of a "blue-chip" stock may be massive and approach the amount of the original investment.

The following chart shows that the annual dividend from the S&P 500 index at the end of 2024 was almost as much as the original investment forty-five years earlier. Some "blue-chip" companies that have increased their dividend consistently, such as Johnson & Johnson, achieved this "breakeven" status in as little as thirty-five years.[61] If you are lucky enough to find the next tech wonder company that pays a dividend, it could possibly happen even faster.[62]

Of course, finding the next emerging growth company early is much more luck than skill. Then again, if you own the types of companies we advocate—financially strong, good return on capital, low debt, modest capital expenditures with loyal customers, and pay a dividend—your chances improve dramatically.

The benefit of owning rising dividend-paying companies is hard to overstate.

---

61 "Johnson & Johnson—63 Year Stock Price History: JNJ," Macrotrends, accessed June 20, 2025, https://www.macrotrends.net/stocks/charts/JNJ/johnson-johnson/stock-price-history.

62 "Microsoft—39 Year Stock Price History: MSFT," Macrotrends, accessed June 20, 2025, https://www.macrotrends.net/stocks/charts/MSFT/microsoft/stock-price-history.

Comparing income-generated bonds and dividend stocks over the long term

Annual dividend income (S&P 500) and interest income (Bloomberg Aggregate)
on $10,000 invested on January 1, 1979 (1979–2023)

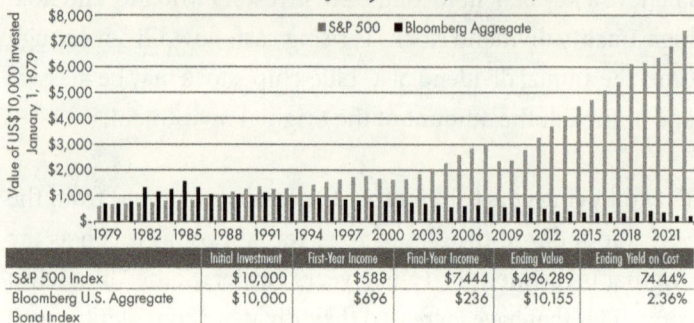

	Initial Investment	First-Year Income	Final-Year Income	Ending Value	Ending Yield on Cost
S&P 500 Index	$10,000	$588	$7,444	$496,289	74.44%
Bloomberg U.S. Aggregate Bond Index	$10,000	$696	$236	$10,155	2.36%

RISING DIVIDENDS, MODERATE PAYOUT

The sweet spot for dividend investing seems to be at the inter-section of companies increasing their dividend and the dividend representing a conservative but meaningful payout and yield.

When selecting dividend-paying stocks, it is important to focus on these critical data points:

- Current yield versus historical average yield
- Dividend payout ratio (dividends per share versus earnings per share)
- Annual earnings growth compared to annual dividend growth

DIVIDENDS CAN BE A DEFENSIVE TOOL

With tens of billions of dollars trading hands every day on the New York Stock Exchange alone, it's easy to lose sight that when purchasing a stock, investors are effectively purchasing owner-ship interest in a business. Assume for a moment that you don't get a quote every day for your shares in that business and that you can't sell your ownership interest for several decades. Your focus would likely shift from the current price of the stock to the value of the business operation. In other words, if the company is satisfying customers and increasing earnings at the same time, its value is appreciating.

The value of that business, whether publicly traded or privately held, is the present value of all future cash flows. After all, what is the point of owning a business—or any investment—if you're never going to receive any cash from it? When a company generates positive free cash flow, it has several options: the company can hold cash in reserve, fund organic growth, make acquisitions, pay down debt, or return it to shareholders through dividends or stock buybacks.

AVERAGE ANNUAL RETURNS AND
VOLATILITY BY DIVIDEND POLICY
S&P 500 INDEX (1973-2024)

	RETURNS	BETA	STANDARD DEVIATION
Dividend Growers & Initiators	10.24%	0.88	16.09%
Dividend Payers	9.20%	0.94	16.84%
No Change in Dividend Policy	6.75%	1.02	18.56%
Dividend Cutters & Eliminators	–0.89%	1.21	24.94%
Dividend Non-Payers	4.31%	1.17	22.06%
Equal-Weighted S&P 500 Index	7.65%	1.00	17.71%

As of 12/31/24. Past performance does not guarantee future results. Indices are unmanaged and not available for direct investment. For illustrative purposes only. Data Sources: Ned Davis Research and Hartford Funds, 3/25.

Investors seeking "growth" might view dividend payments negatively. Their logic being that if the business is generating high rates of return on capital, all cash flows should be reinvested in the business. That makes complete sense. However, it is almost impossible to know how long that will continue to be the case, and the stock price volatility tends to be higher.[63]

In a more risk-averse investing climate, dividend payments potentially offer an advantageous method of returning value to shareholders. Shareholders, just like any owner, should be concerned with maximizing long-term value, not short-term earnings.

As indicated earlier, there will be times when non-dividend-paying stocks outperform dividend-paying stocks. Akin to the "Go Go" years of the late 60s, both the dot.com stocks in the 90's and the FAANG stocks well outperformed dividend-paying stocks.[64] However, most people forget about when the Magnificent Seven went down 39.9 percent in 2022.[65] After you go down 39.9 percent, you have to go up 65 percent to break even.

After the dot-com bubble burst, the S&P 500 experienced a "lost decade," with the average starting and ending at a modest

---

63   "Is Dividend Investing Worth It? The Complete Guide," Saratoga Investment Corp., accessed June 20, 2025, https://saratogainvestmentcorp.com/articles/is-dividend-investing-worth-it-the-complete-guide/.

64   Kenneth Silber, "The Go-Go Sixties," ThinkAdvisor, April 1, 2008, https://www.thinkadvisor.com/2008/04/01/the-go-go-sixties/.

65   Andrei Senyuk, "Measuring the Impact of the Magnificent Seven on Market Returns with Syntax Direct," Research, Syntax, October 17, 2024, https://www.syntaxdata.com/research/measuring-the-impact-of-the-magnificent-seven-on-market-returns-with-syntax-direct.

loss.[66] Only time will tell if the decade following the Magnificent Seven period will have a similar "lost decade."[67]

Dividend Investing: Simple, Yet Not Easy

Dividend investing is not as simple as selecting the highest yielding stock with the fastest short-term dividend growth. Fundamental analysis is required to avoid regrettable mistakes. At times, some companies initiate dividends in the hopes of attracting investors. Avoid those that borrow to pay the dividend or grow their dividends faster than earnings. Neither is sustainable.

Historically, owning stocks that pay dividends with conservative payout ratios and increasing yields offers value in any environment. The cash flow buffers the stock price in bear markets, the dividend presents new cash that can be reinvested at lower prices, and the greater stability allows you to allocate higher percentages to stocks instead of bonds or cash.

Most importantly, owning assets with rising income allows me to sleep well at night and gives me peace of mind.

After all, that's all that matters.

---

66 Noel Watson, "The S&P 500 Lost Decade—How to Protect Your Retirement," *Pyrford Financial Planning* (blog), last updated June 22, 2025, https://www.pyrfordfp.com/post/the-s-p-500-lost-decade-how-to-protect-your-retirement.

67 The "Magnificent Seven" is taken from the 1960 movie of the same name and refers to seven of the largest companies in the S&P 500 index: Microsoft, Apple, Nvidia, Amazon, Meta, Alphabet, and Tesla.

Summary

1. Assets with rising income, such as real estate or common stocks, are preferred. Dividends have been an important part of total return.

2. High dividends and rising dividends are different. Companies with high dividends may have low or no growth. Dividend-paying stocks have outpaced the performance of non-dividend-paying stocks—and with lower volatility.[68]

3. The best time to invest for rising dividends is today. The time to get a great price for a company might be when that company is out of favor.

Next Chapter

1. The next chapter explores "sudden wealth syndrome," an expression used to describe people who suddenly come into large sums of money, whether through inheritance or by selling a company. Learning how to handle sudden wealth can be daunting.

2. Sudden wealth can have a significant effect on the suddenly wealthy and those around them. Take your time, get organized, and avoid the urge to splurge.

3. Create future streams of income and protect yourself from predators of all types. My best advice? Go slow.

---

68   Chris Gallant, "Why Are Dividend-Paying Stocks Less Volatile?," Investopedia, last updated May 15, 2022, https://www.investopedia.com/ask/answers/06/pricevolatilitydividendsvsnodividends.asp.

CHAPTER 13

YOU JUST CAME INTO A PILE OF MONEY, NOW WHAT?

I regularly encounter people coming into the unfamiliar responsibility of overseeing significant wealth. This is usually because they sold a business or received a large inheritance. For illustration's sake, let's assume their new wealth totals more than $20 million, maybe a lot more. The question that looms large is where to start.

In order to start, you need to know where you are, where you want to go, and then how to get there. My first recommendation is not to jump right into investing. Start with a personal financial statement.

||||||||

A personal financial statement is a document,
not a $10 million house or $400,000 car.

||||||||

The temptation is to splurge, and that's fine, within reason. Just be sure you don't spend too much too soon and end up with headaches and hassles from a collection of assets that may quickly feel like liabilities. For example, flush with a lot of cash, some people go out and buy vacation homes, expensive cars, and even private planes. Later, when the cost of insuring, using, and maintaining these new possessions become evident, they often turn around and sell the "trophy" assets at a substantial loss.

Down the road, you will need to think about how to protect these assets from spurious claims by former partners or spouses, managers, employees, etc. Depending on the amount of publicity surrounding the liquidity event (that is, the sale of the company or property or the estate transfer), you may find yourself targeted for theft or cyber attacks. For now, just getting the basic legal structures, obtaining insurance, and paying any applicable taxes is enough.

Be Happy, Don't Stress

Priorities and to-do lists, goals and action plans, schedules and milestones fill our days and our lives. None of that makes us happy, so take a moment and start with the basics.

Define success. Most people think of success as being connected with their family and community, feeling secure about the future, and having the time and resources to help others. So how do we achieve these amid our hectic day-to-day lives? A few thoughts to consider:

1. *Start each day being grateful* for the people you have in your life. This will bring peace and balance to your thinking. It will also condition your mind to see the good and even find the benefits of setbacks.
2. *Focus on the important things* that will bring great joy—things like spending more time with family or friends and mentoring and helping others achieve their dreams. Odds are high you will focus on your family first, and somewhere down the list will come your finances.
3. *Write letters* to your spouse, partner, family, friends, and/or children to let them know how much you love and appreciate them. It is a gift that will last a lifetime.

Okay, now for the money part.

Family First, Finances Follow

Any serious discussion about managing wealth has to start with its larger purpose, and that invariably begins with your family. From my perspective, accumulating financial assets is not the ultimate goal. Financial assets are tools to help accomplish personal goals.

Spend an hour with your spouse or partner and write down your thoughts to align with each other. This step is powerful and very important, yet it is surprising how infrequently it is done.

- Values, philosophies, or beliefs. What do you want your grandchildren to know about you?
- Life and family goals
- Financial goals
- Community or philanthropic goals

Compare notes and work toward a common list for your family. This conversation should help ensure you are starting on the same page, heading in the same direction, and happy about where you want to end up. When you are in agreement, the rest of the process goes more smoothly.

Cash Flow Is King

On a simple spreadsheet, prepare a personal financial statement or have your CPA do it for you. This is to determine how much cash you can expect to generate to support your lifestyle and keep your expenses in line. Your personal financial statement should include your assets, liabilities, and net worth. Categorize the assets by legal owner, who controls it, and where it is custodied.

Everyone with wealth needs financial and estate plans, but in the first year or two of your new-found wealth, they don't have to be in great detail. Too many people start the planning process only to abandon it because of the time and complexity required. To start, you only need to know the basics: how much cash flow do you need to live a "normal," comfortable life, and will the income come from royalties, consulting fees, dividends from stocks, rental real estate, or other sources?

Organize Important Documents

Organize your wills, estate plans, powers of attorney, medical proxies, final directives, etc. Know the locations of insurance policies, company ownership agreements, partnership documents, and trust paperwork. You will want to revisit these with your advisors soon, but locating them is the first step.

With your goals aligned, documents organized, and cash flow needs understood, you can better know what you need to do. Congratulations—this alone puts you far ahead of most people. The question to ask now is, "Should I seek a wealth advisor to help us do all this, or do I want to do it alone?"

Using a Wealth Advisor or Going It Alone, Questions to Ask:

You may assume I am going to recommend using an advisor—and you are right. But it only makes sense if you know what is being done for you—that is, the services rendered—and understand the value versus the expense. Questions you might ask include:

- How will the advisor alleviate the majority of the hassles associated with managing wealth?
- Does the advisor have a network of qualified accoun-

tants, tax advisors, attorneys, and insurance brokers so you don't have to source and interview dozens of providers personally?

- Can the advisor help you to think about asset allocation outside of stocks, bonds, and liquid investments? Real estate? Investments in private companies?
- What experience does the advisor have with specialty items (offshore trust and tax, private placement insurance, dynasty trusts, kidnap and ransom insurance, crypto cold storage, and philanthropic management)?
- Will you earn above-average investment returns? This is a trick question. Be leery of advisors who exude too much confidence about "beating" the stock market. As you know, it is very hard to do.

To me, it is a no-brainer. Once you have achieved this level of wealth, do you want to tether yourself to a desk, taking on risk and worry, for the possibility of adding incremental value? In my opinion, engaging a qualified advisor to assist you in managing your family's wealth will save you thousands of hours and almost certainly lots of money.

Summary

1. Once you are wealthy, you don't need to show it or prove anything. Wait a while, and get used to having wealth.

2. You can always make a big splash later. For a year or two at least, maintain a low profile.

3. The pressure to do things, go places, accept invitations, join clubs, and invest in once-in-a-lifetime deals may be overwhelming. Say no to almost everything.

Next Chapter

1. The next chapter describes the beginning of the journey to financial freedom through investing. For those just starting out and investing to accumulate wealth, hope for an extended bear market. Embrace bear markets by investing the same amount of money every month, also known as "dollar cost averaging."

2. When you invest as market values decline, you accumulate more shares at lower prices. When the economy and markets rebound, as they always have, your rainy-day fund may resemble Noah's Ark.

3. Buy quality, collect income, and hold for a long time.

CHAPTER 14

HOW YOUNG PEOPLE MAY ACHIEVE FINANCIAL INDEPENDENCE

The son of a client called me to discuss how to invest his savings. We discussed the basics—save, invest, repeat. Then, we spoke about the ways to do it. In his case, he wanted to own individual stocks, so I asked him to write a journal of what he wanted to buy and why. I also asked him when he might want to sell it and why. From experience, I can tell you that the overwhelming majority of professional advisors I know do not do that for themselves, nor do their clients. It is so basic, and yet so few do it.

This man was different—he did it. He is unusually diligent, and we still have regular conversations about his accumulating net worth. I told him and his new bride they could achieve financial independence not because of the portfolio returns, although they will likely be good, but because of his approach, maturity, and patience.

I have seen a lot of approaches to building investment portfolios in the last forty years. The three ways most people start building portfolios are systematic purchases, valuation, and market timing. Two work; one doesn't.[69]

STARTING OUT

For most investors of relatively modest means, systematic purchases of well-known, global, blue-chip stocks, also known as "dollar cost averaging," is the way to go. You set up a diversified portfolio that you regularly acquire over the years, staying the course during booms and busts because you have neither the experience nor time to manage a portfolio yourself.

One form of systematic purchases would be putting several hundred dollars a month into multiple stocks until you end up with a portfolio of blue-chip companies with dividend income. As to which companies to buy, I prefer higher-quality companies that have certain advantages protecting them from competition and technological changes.

---

69   Sheena Hanson, "10 Benefits of Dollar Cost Averaging (DCA) as an Investment Strategy," *Financial Planning* (blog), Uncommon Cents Investing, October 19, 2023, https://uncommoncentsinvesting.com/financial-planning/dollar-cost-averaging-dca-investing-guide/; Katelyn Peters, "Market Timing: What It Is and How It Can Backfire," Investopedia, last updated August 26, 2024, https://www.investopedia.com/terms/m/markettiming.asp.

ADOPT A "REAL ESTATE" MINDSET

Successful owners of real estate look for good properties in good locations with good tenants. In common stock terms, think of that as owning "blue-chip" companies with global brands run by management teams with histories of increasing earnings with modest capital expenditures. In other words, think of yourself as being in the business of acquiring dividends that will go up in the future. Most people assume rent from real estate will go up a little each year.[70] The same assumption can be made with many stocks.[71]

Of all the ways to reach your financial goals, systematic investing is one of the least risky if—and this is a big if—you are willing and able to hold onto your companies for at least twenty-five years.[72] You must be willing to hold on, even if we go into a full-blown Great Depression.

TIMING INVESTMENTS

Benjamin Graham, the father of investing, observed that most investors under most circumstances should not worry about trying to get the best price when buying stock.[73] History has proven him right, especially for truly excellent businesses, if you stretch the ownership period out long enough. Even the Nifty

---

70 Vincent Diaz, "Is Real Estate an Inflation Hedge? Looking at Historical Trends," *Vaster* (blog), September 4, 2024, https://blog.vaster.com/real-estate-inflation-hedge.

71 Matthew J. Bartolini and Sri Burra, "The Value of Dividend Growth Strategies to Portfolios Today and Beyond," Insights, State Street Investment Management, April 11, 2025, https://www.ssga.com/us/en/intermediary/insights/the-value-of-dividend-growth-strategies-to-portfolios-today-and-beyond.

72 Jeremy J. Siegel, "The Nifty-Fifty Revisited: Do Growth Stocks Ultimately Justify Their Price," *Journal of Portfolio Management* 21, no. 4 (Summer 1995): 8–20, DOI: 10.3905/jpm.1995.8.

73 Benjamin Graham, *The Intelligent Investor*, rev. ed. (HarperBusiness Essentials, 2003), 8.

Fifty ended up beating the S&P 500 a quarter-century later despite several bankruptcies of components along the way.[74]

Even with an occasional failure, the success of the survivors more than makes up for any losses. One might make the argument that as long as you are not investing more than 2 percent to 5 percent portfolio weighting of any one stock and you truly will hold for twenty-five years, even if we go into a 1929–1933 catastrophe, there may rarely be a bad time to buy certain "blue-chip" companies.

EXPECT AND EMBRACE VOLATILITY

For those with a long time horizon, especially younger people, look forward to the next time the broad stock market goes down in price by 20 to 25 percent. This is your golden chance to buy more of your favorite cash machines at lower prices. Too often, the media scares people into a panic, and many investors sell at lower prices. Remember this: stock markets go up and down 15 to 20 percent virtually every year.[75]

When it comes to individual companies, most of your holdings could increase or decrease peak to trough by at least 33 percent every thirty-six months. That is normal.[76] If you buy a great business as part of a diversified portfolio and pay a fair price for

---

74   "Revisiting the Nifty Fifty," Stray Reflections, May 16, 2022, https://stray-reflections.com/articles/history/revisiting-the-nifty-fifty.

75   Scott R. Baker et al., "Equity Market Volatility Tracker: Overall," Federal Reserve Bank of St. Louis, accessed June 20, 2025, https://fred.stlouisfed.org/series/EMVOVERALLEMV.

76   C. Thomas Howard, "Unlocking Stock Market Success: Why You Should Embrace the Skew," *Enterprising Investor* (blog), CFA Institute, October 23, 2024, https://blogs.cfainstitute.org/investor/2024/10/23/unlocking-stock-market-success-why-you-should-embrace-the-skew/.

it, it shouldn't cause concern if you wake up to find the price down a third from where you bought it.

Why Being Patient Matters

It is difficult to emphasize enough the importance of patience. Look at the length of time Warren Buffett held the most profitable stocks in Berkshire Hathaway. Most of the real money he made came from investments made more than a quarter century before. These stakes generated billions upon billions in after-tax dividends that funded other, newer investments.[77] Some holding periods are now surpassing the fifty-year mark.

Warren Buffett has long espoused that by making only twenty investment decisions in a forty-year career, you would make better decisions and much more money. Charlie Munger said he and Warren made most of their money by sitting on their hands doing "nothing." Learning to say no to most things is a very valuable skill.

Should I Buy More on Dips?

A small percentage of investors take a hybrid approach between systematic purchases and valuation, so it is not an all-or-nothing deal. For example, investors who increased the amount they were putting into their 401(k) in 2008–2009, when the stock market had fallen, believed stock prices were more attractive at the time. Same thing in March and April of 2020. They de

---

77   Warren E. Buffett, *Berkshire Hathaway 2016 Shareholder Letter* (Berkshire Hathaway, 2016), 2–29, https://www.berkshirehathaway.com/letters/2016ltr.pdf.

facto ended up accelerating their own recovery time by buying more shares at lower prices.

"My advisor said don't panic, I'm still young enough to recoup my losses."

DOES IT EVER MAKE SENSE TO SELL?

Of course. If you need the money, have cash on hand well before you need it. From an investment perspective, yes, at times, stocks can become so highly valued it makes sense to sell. Even admired CEOs have admitted to their shareholders it was a mistake not to sell Coca-Cola when it had a stock price more than fifty times its recent earnings. For an established company like Coca-Cola, that was a very high valuation.[78] The answer for high-quality companies at really high valuations is, occasionally, you should sell, but not often.

The real question when considering selling is what to do with the proceeds. The way the math works, you have to be pretty sure the new investment will generate a return that is about 50 percent better than what you already have. If the only thing that has changed with a good-quality asset is that the price went up, be slow to sell.

What About Selling Everything?

Very rarely, if ever, will you sell everything. Maybe once or twice in a lifetime, and even then, probably not everything. It is exceedingly hard to know when to sell and when to buy back in. One example was a period during the dot-com boom when Vanguard's founder, John Bogle, liquidated something like all but the last 35 percent of his stock and equity index fund investments, putting it all, instead, into cash, Treasury securities, and bonds. The valuation gap (meaning the difference between historical valuation and the then-current valuation) had become so large that he talked about it being a once-in-a-generation disconnect he could no longer ignore; he threw the "stay the course" mantra of systematic investing out the window. He was right.[79]

78   Warren Buffet, "Warren Buffett Regrets Not Selling Coca Cola at 50x Earnings," clip from panel discussion, Thomas Chua, YouTube video, 2:14, https://www.youtube.com/watch?v=oWpXM3sVAek.

79   Jack Bogle, "Jack Bogle on Asset Allocation and Market Collapse (2014)," clip from interview, Mark White, YouTube video, 13:55, https://www.youtube.com/watch?v=k6ra5POdsYg.

Plan, Don't React

To an investor, the market price is there to be exploited or ignored. As Benjamin Graham put it in his book *The Intelligent Investor*:[80]

> The most realistic distinction between the investor and the speculator is found in their attitude toward stock-market movements. The speculator's primary interest lies in anticipating and profiting from market fluctuations. The investor's primary interest lies in acquiring and holding suitable securities at suitable prices.

Patient Investing Helps Drive Wealth Accumulation

In my opinion, passivity is much more effective than trading when it comes to accumulating wealth. You only have to make two correct decisions: which asset to acquire, and the price you want to pay. Then, you sit back and enjoy the fruits it produces decade after decade. Trying to predict what any firm's stock price will do in the short term (a.k.a. market timing) cannot be done consistently.

Under extreme conditions, such as the Great Depression, if you were able to hold on to your stocks, you broke even and then made money. For those who were able to reinvest their dividends through the Great Depression, their break-even was less than five years because they bought so many more shares at such low prices.[81] Under most economic scenarios, a twenty-

---

80 Graham, *Intelligent Investor*, 205.

81 Mark Hulbert, "25 Years to Bounce Back? Try 4 ½," *New York Times*, April 25, 2009, https://www.nytimes.com/2009/04/26/your-money/stocks-and-bonds/26stra.html.

five-year holding period should be highly satisfactory for the prices you are likely to pay.

SUMMARY

1. Buy quality, invest systematically, and embrace "sell-offs" and economic downturns. No matter how bad it seems, it always gets better.

2. Arrange your portfolio so the risks are tolerable. Add to your regular savings pattern when market values go down.

3. Think long term, sit tight, and avoid the temptation to "do something."

NEXT CHAPTER

1. The next chapter explains that more money has been made by "not losing it" than one can ever know. A large part of not losing money is simply avoiding speculation and trading. The message is simple: Just Say No.

2. Every day, someone tries to sell someone else a great idea. Most aren't.

3. Know what the ideal investment looks like. Decline to invest in anything less.

CHAPTER 15

||||||||||

SECRET TO STAYING RICH: JUST SAY NO

The Best Trade I Ever Did Was the One I Never Did

For five years, I was on the Citigroup Global Capital Commitment Committee. Capital commitment committees exist to ensure the securities underwritten by a firm and offered to the public have followed the rules and regulations. If a firm underwrites a security and things go poorly, the reputation of the underwriter is harmed, and legal damages may result.

In the process of approving the investment bank's underwriting, I spent most of my time learning what mistakes to avoid. One of my mentors was a lawyer who started his career in the "reorganization department." That is the group that attempts to resolve bad loans before they go into bankruptcy. His early training was seeing the mistakes, oversights, and poor judgments of others. He taught me how to look for low-probability financial problems that might occur: the proverbial dog who should have barked.

It was this training that led me and another person to prevent two toxic products, collateralized mortgage obligations and collateralized loan obligations (CMOs and CLOs), from being sold to individual clients at Citigroup Smith Barney.[82] In 2008 and 2009, when so many sophisticated investors lost hundreds of millions of dollars buying these risky securities, private clients of Citigroup Smith Barney were spared. In the investment business, there is a saying, "The best trade you ever did was the one you never did."

When we did not allow those products to be sold to retail clients, we were effectively saying no to the head of the Fixed Income Department, one of the highest-paid and most-powerful senior executives in Citi. The decision carried career risk, but it was the right thing to do. Fortunately, I had a great boss who provided me with the "air cover" to survive the inevitable criticism from the people whose revenue was crimped. Learning to say no saved a lot of people a lot of money. It almost cost me my job.

ALWAYS INVERT: HOW TO AVOID BECOMING POOR

I love Charlie Munger's maxim "Always invert." This means to consider the opposite perspective to see clearly. In this case, if we want to learn how to get rich, the first step is to understand how to avoid becoming poor.

Everyone studies how families got rich. People have also studied how families became poor. The surprising fact is that when families go from wealthy to poor, it isn't always because they spent

---

82   These were the products featured in Michael Lewis' 2010 book, *The Big Short*. In the 2015 movie adaptation of Lewis's book, Ryan Gosling explains how they work using a Jenga tower.

too much money. Yes, new wealth entices people to buy boats, planes, and baubles only to sell them at some future time at half the price. That happens. Less obvious is the accumulation of poor investment decisions that drain balance sheets.

My experience shows that a great deal of money has been lost—or, to put it more bluntly, wasted—by investing in unproven businesses, trophy projects like movie deals or Broadway plays, speculative land deals, and loans to relatives. It is understandable that people will want to spend their newfound money on "shiny objects." But, from an investment perspective, all these things should be avoided.

"Try this. My broker said it could double."

Clients who want to stay wealthy should not invest in most of the "opportunities" presented to them. I encourage clients to limit their nontraditional investments to no more than one per year. This discipline may seem arbitrary or extreme. On the other hand, making frequent decisions reduces the amount of time available to research and consider. If you can only invest in one or two things every few years, the odds are much higher that you will weigh the decisions more closely and make better decisions.

In the last chapter, I noted how Buffett and Munger made most of their money by saying no to opportunities. Over time, I have found that when I said no to various deals, often they would later come back to me at better prices and under more favorable terms.

Sometimes, the best advice I can give is *Just Say No.*

Summary

1. Expecting the best is good. Dedicate time to considering the things that could go wrong before investing. Understanding what may go wrong can "save your bacon."

2. Understanding how families go broke is just as important as learning how they got rich.

3. The best time to invest is not when you have money. The best time to invest is when others don't.

Next Chapter

1. At my firm, Promethium Advisors, we follow all the advice in this book, and yet how we implement these principles when investing is different than many. This is not the only way to invest and may not be the "best" way. It is just our way.

2. We invest taxable assets for long-term growth, seeking companies that can be held for decades. At times, we have high conviction in trends that can lead to a large percentage of our assets being concentrated in a few industries or companies.

3. The next chapter is more of a mindset than a guide and touches on the few ways we invest differently. There is no assurance we will have higher returns nor do we encourage others to attempt this on their own.

CHAPTER 16

||||||||||

PORTFOLIO MANAGEMENT

"I have nothing to add."

Before his death in November of 2023, the most common response from former Vice Chairman of Berkshire Hathaway Charles T. Munger was succinct and to the point.

To the casual observer, it may appear that Charlie didn't have much to add.

To those who study how the great investors of our time arrived at their decisions, we know better. Charlie was in a league of his own.

To oversimplify his process, Charlie used a series of eighty or more mental models across more than twenty disciplines to first assess the logic of a situation, then overlay the psychological factors contributing to it, and finally assess the likely misjudgments that led to the situation.

If this sounds complicated and difficult, it is. Knowing what to do is difficult. Knowing how to do it is more difficult. Doing it well is nearly impossible for most.

How I Manage Money

This chapter has been saved for last in this section because what follows is a description of how I have come to manage my own money and the money of Promethium's clients. Most financial advisors buy mutual funds or ETFs or recommend separately managed accounts. We at Promethium Advisors buy individual stocks. Many advisors ignore tax consequences, while others employ automated ETF trading programs. We are tax-sensitive and very tactical with how we manage the tax impact.

Our way is not the only way nor do we claim it is the best way. It is simply "our" way. If we have any advantages over other approaches, which we might not, they could be our longer vision, desire to own quality, and preference to invest early and hold for years.[83] We tend to take our time arriving at decisions, attempt to stay dispassionate about market volatility, and are willing to go on record with our views. None of this ensures better results, but we believe it reduces the frequency and magnitude of avoidable mistakes.

---

83 When we refer to "quality," we mean investments that are strong financially and have good reputations. This usually implies modest debt, loyal customers, and predictable cash flow, which normally, but not always, leads to rising income.

ISO compounders. Our goal is to find and buy companies that can consistently generate free cash flow for many years. We call them "cash flow compounding machines." They are hard to find and even harder to find at attractive prices. When they surface, they are usually disguised in an ugly exterior. When we own one, it is hard to buy more at "higher" prices, and the urge to sell and claim victory is even harder to suppress. While some investors advocate trading in and out of stocks and bonds and others trade in and out of "growth" or "value" stocks, when we find companies that are well positioned and well managed, we tend to hold on to them.

EVALUATING COMPANIES

The following are the attributes we seek when investing in companies.

FINANCIAL STRENGTH

In order to succeed, you must first survive. We tend to attempt to help mitigate risk by owning companies with strong balance sheets. We want companies whose survival should not be threatened by recessions, interruptions, or geopolitical events. Make no mistake, they will be impacted, but their ability to endure should not be in question.

RETURN ON CAPITAL

A good business deploys capital wisely and generates profits. We prefer to own companies with above-average returns on capital. We avoid businesses that (1) sell price-sensitive products, (2) require continual large investments in equipment, or

(3) are overly sensitive to energy or labor price swings. Cyclical companies can be wonderful investments if you buy and sell them at the right prices. This is hard to do.

Debt to Equity

Businesses with strong earnings-growth prospects often use debt to grow. Generally, this works in most cases, as long as the borrowed funds are put to productive use. Companies with long histories should have a better sense for when and how debt should be used. Younger companies with newer management and new products have a history of optimism, which usually is met with disappointment. Balancing the proper amount of debt and how to use it is part art and part prudence.

Capital Expenditures

Businesses that do not require significant ongoing investment are preferred. Heavy industry and manufacturing normally require a lot of cash flow to be reinvested to stay competitive. Companies with "free" cash flow can invest in areas that can expand the business, pay down debt, buy back stock, or pay dividends.

Rising Free Cash Flow

Companies with a history of higher return on capital that have rising free cash flow are on the road to higher dividends, stock price increases, and shareholder loyalty. Free cash flow is the amount of money a company has left after earning profits and paying taxes. Think about it like the amount of money you have at the end of the year after you have paid all your bills and funded your 401(k) to the max; it is the money left over. Rising free cash flow offers the choice to deploy funds intelligently by investing in new products or machinery, expanding a territory, or increasing the dividend.

With the right management team, rising free cash flow offers nearly infinite opportunity. It is hard to imagine we would own a company that did not have the prospect of rising free cash flow in the near future.

Management

One of the most difficult aspects to assess is the intangible quality of management. Good management ensures the common shareholder is treated fairly. Great management treats shareholders like the C-suite. This is exceedingly difficult to find. Some say that, ideally, you want to own a company that can survive bad management because eventually it will suffer from it. We agree but would prefer to start off on the right foot. Alignment of economic interests with a management team we feel we can trust tilts the scale in favor of the shareholder.

Power in Concentration

We structure portfolios with reasonable diversification, twenty-five to thirty-five stocks, and yet we are willing to let a great company compound into a large percent of the overall portfolio. At times, some portfolios become more concentrated than many textbooks suggest is wise. For example, if a company starts out with a 3 percent weighting and increases in price from five to fifty, most textbooks would suggest you sell the position (probably at twenty). For those who have owned the great growth companies of the last forty years, their net worth might be a fraction of what it is today had they blindly followed that advice.

Textbooks that recommend frequent rebalancing (meaning selling assets that significantly rose in value to buy assets that did not) may be appropriate for nontaxable accounts that seek lower volatility. If the objective of the fund is to minimize volatility, it pays no taxes on gains, and it is subjected to an investment committee's scrutiny every quarter, this makes complete sense.

When managing taxable portfolios, on the other hand, we seek after-tax wealth accumulation over many years. While we do not believe we are likely to find the next company that goes up one hundred times over the next twenty years, if I own a company that may become important to millions or even billions of customers, I won't sell it just to satisfy an arbitrary metric over an arbitrary timeframe.

Selling

We do not trade frequently but do occasionally employ "tax-loss harvesting." Tax-loss harvesting is the practice of selling at a loss to maximize tax deductions. Selling a stock when the price is lower than what I paid requires me to admit I was wrong and made a mistake. Human nature can lead us to look for excuses outside our control to explain why the price went down and for reasons why the stock will rise and I will be proven correct. I have found this thinking to be costly.

Many times, we have bought a stock, watched it fall, and sold it at a loss with the idea of rebuying it thirty-two days later, after the "wash sale" period expires.[84] Then, when the "wash sale" period was over, we decided not to rebuy it. Forgive me for using jargon, as some of the terms are tax and investing related, while others are related to human behavior.

To be a good portfolio manager, one must be able to limit the normal emotions that can compel the average investor to make costly mistakes. Studies suggest that, done properly, tax-loss harvesting adds value. It also breaks our anchoring bias, meaning once we have made a decision, we will do almost anything possible not to change our mind and admit we were wrong.

Valuing Intangibles

One of the key things to keep in mind is the value of intangibles. In accounting terms, they can be "goodwill" or intellectual property. In non-accounting terms, they are things like reputation and trust. All iconic brands—car makers, enduring fashion labels, mobile phones, a discount warehouse, or an Omaha-based insurance company—have intangible value. Most people understand this, and yet our human nature, especially those quantitatively oriented, prefer order and "proof." Having facts and data is comforting when our investments don't work out. A key to successful portfolio management is correctly estimating how much an unobservable intangible is worth. I claim no extraordinary ability to discern this; I only know how important it can be.

---

84   A wash sale occurs when you sell securities at a loss and then buy them back within thirty days of the sale. IRS rules prohibit you from deducting losses related to wash sales.

Challenge: We Overvalue Easily Observed Data

What is the value of customer loyalty?

How to solve for this?

Price—Earnings Ratio

Costco

Fair Value

Return

Time

ALIGNMENT OF INTERESTS

I like investing in companies with managers who have a significant amount of their own money invested on the same terms as mine. This goes for general partners of real estate and private equity as well. Principals who manage clients' assets the way they manage their own and have real skin in the game are the partners I seek.

The vast majority of investment opportunities are structured with very little of the organizer's personal money at risk. For example, most public-company executives have generous option packages, creating incentives but not alignment. The executive is incentivized to increase the stock price, sometimes by taking risk or using debt. When things work out, the investor does well, and the executive does very well. However, if things do not go well, the investor loses their money, while the executive only loses upside. To have true alignment, both the executive and investor would lose money if things go poorly. This creates better corporate behavior and, in my opinion, improves our risk–reward equation.

This chapter admittedly is brief because the purpose of the book is to share what I have learned from advising the very wealthy about money and meaning. Money by itself doesn't deliver happiness nor give meaning to our lives. Money gives us the means to make an impact. It is the positive impact we weave into the lives of others that is truly lasting and worth pursuing.

|||||||||

"When you know yourself and what is good,
your choices become clear."
—Plato

|||||||||

On the Record

Publishing investment commentary improves the clarity of my thinking and informs clients about how I attempt to protect their money and why we own the stocks we own. When investing, maintaining a journal of what you believe, why you believe it, and the outcomes you anticipate will keep you honest. When I am wrong, which, like most investors, is often, I look back to see what I missed and try to evaluate why. Only by keeping scrupulous details about successes and failures can I hope to improve and lessen the chances of repeating past mistakes.

Summary

1. I seek to own profitable companies with strong financials, rising cash flow, and loyal customers. Ideally, I like to buy them after a correctable problem has made their price attractive.

2. I prefer to own assets for a long time to allow compounding to occur.

3. I communicate my views about what I believe might happen in the future and how I position my money and my clients' money to clarify my thinking and evaluate decisions.

Next Section

1. The final section addresses a handful of topics centered around family communication. I first focus on communicating through better listening.

2. The second and third chapters involve preparing the next generation. The second is about preparing them for the responsibilities of overseeing wealth. The third is about handling a tricky situation: discussing prenuptial agreements.

3. The last chapter is on communicating with aging parents when it is time for them to "give up the keys," whether they be to the car or the checkbook. Easing the burden of aging through dignified transitions is what everyone wants.

PART III

MANAGING TRANSITIONS

Sometime today, think about the people in your life who provided the rivets and the ladders, call them up, and tell them you too will "love them forever."

That was the final line of my mother's eulogy. My father had died two years earlier, and my siblings asked me to deliver the final tribute. As the oldest son, I felt a sense of responsibility. It was not a weight; it was life.

I spoke about the rivets of a steel bridge, almost invisible to see yet without which there would be no structure. That was my mother—she held our family together. I spoke about ladders, the help we receive throughout our lives, and our opportunities to help others.

My concluding line referenced a childhood book, *I'll Love You Forever*, in which, at the outset, the son is held by his mother, and at the end, the mother is held by her son. Life transitions occur every day. Some are unexpected, some are not fun, but most are inevitable. It is up to all of us to prepare for and embrace them, whatever they may be.

The title of this book, *Money and Meaning*, conveys there is much more to life than managing money and accumulating wealth.

Managing transitions gets to the meaning part, which to most is far more important than the money part. Once you have done all the money things correctly, you want to ensure you pass along values, purpose, and stewardship when assuming the reins or giving them to others.

To increase the chances of others following my advice, I start with effective communication through listening. It probably took me forty years before I understood that *effective* communication does not start with oratory skills; it starts with *listening*. The first chapter of this section discusses what I have learned about listening and being truly heard.

In the next chapter, transitioning responsibility and authority to the next generation with patience and process is explored. Though this has been a challenge for parents and their children since biblical times, I offer a few tactics to consider as you navigate your situation.

Finally, I touch on communicating with maturing children and aging parents. These topics can be tricky, and thinking about them in advance can lead to smoother outcomes. My intent is to offer thoughts on how to maintain healthy personal relationships while dispensing thoughtful advice and financial protection.

No two situations are identical, and every situation takes time. With love and patience, everything is possible.

CHAPTER 17

||||||||||

SACRED ART OF LISTENING

Epiphany: It's Not All About Me

I was attending a function where the format was short videos followed by small group discussions. After a half dozen sessions, I had become less enthusiastic because I wasn't getting much out of the sessions. Over the course of a few weeks, the post-video conversations had veered toward topics that were not that interesting to me.

Out of nowhere, it occurred to me that maybe, just maybe, I shouldn't focus on what I was getting out of the sessions. Maybe I should focus on what I could be giving. I realized the gift I could give was not a pearl of wisdom—it was to simply listen to others.

BACK TO BASICS

In order to be heard, we must first learn to listen. Those who are thoughtful about structuring their wealth and smart about managing money will probably end up with a lot of it. At some point, everything we have will belong to someone else. Therefore, to be effective at managing the transition, we must first learn to listen in order to be heard.

At first glance, this chapter may not make much sense in a book about managing wealth and money. However, having wealth and wisdom without being able to pass it along to family, friends, community, or society is a waste. Receiving a deed to a property or a large check that will clear will always be gladly accepted; however, one of the greatest gifts we can bestow to others is our full attention.

Being in the "advice-giving business" since the day I graduated from college, I have always been "selling." Unfortunately, most of us were trained to talk, not listen. For years, I was the one who waited for others to inhale so I could break the stream of their thought and redirect the conversation to a story that included me or raised me in their esteem. I was that person, the one who thought of myself as a clever raconteur. Sadly, from time to time, I still catch myself in that all-too-common trap.

OVERCOMING HABITS

Then one day, I met someone who really listened. They listened with their eyes and their body. They nodded with energy. They "leaned-in" as they paid attention. They listened until I stopped talking. Then, they repeated what I said and encouraged me to go on. I was so enthused about the attention I didn't realize what was happening until later. This world-class conversation-alist was really just a world-class listener. It was only then I realized that I had a gift I could offer others. I could listen.

In order to really listen, one must pay full attention to the speaker. This does not come naturally to most. Normally, when another person is speaking, most people are preparing their response. I would be thinking how I could relate the topic to a previous experience or share some insight. In short, I wasn't listening.

If I was really going to hear what was being said, I had to avoid thinking about what I was going to say in my response. This is really hard. I had considered myself a good listener when, in fact, I was only half listening. And the half that I missed may have been the most important part.

Managing transitions requires relationships. Healthy relation-ships that lead to effective transitions require listening.

A NEW START

After the meeting where I realized a gift I could give was to pay attention, I started listening to people. It was hard. I had to con-sciously try to hear what was being said—and not being said. I tried to hear the experience and all the facts that surrounded the story. I tried to suspend response, judgment, and association. I tried to suppress identifying with the person and just let their words settle. I tried to let them have the next word, even after it felt like they were done talking. Often, they weren't.

I found myself asking, "What else?" "Tell me more," or "How

did that happen?" I wasn't hiding from speaking; I was giving what most people don't get very often, at least not from me. I was giving my full attention.

Some in the advice-giving business may feel that the more we say, the smarter other people will think we are. Yet, the reality is people understand the depth of our knowledge by the questions we ask, not by the statements we make. With family and friends, the simple act of asking a question and creating a safe environment for something sensitive to be shared can be far more valuable than money.

Become a Better Listener

To manage transitions from your parents and eventually to your children, or to help others manage their own transitions, listen. Make it your goal to be able to repeat back to the speaker what you heard. Focus on what is being said, wait for the silence to fill the space, and wait for the speaker to continue. Ask them to tell you more.

This is not being insincere. It is caring; it is a rare gift. Odds are high you will learn more about the person speaking and, in the process, improve your relationship with them.

What's in it for you? The immediate positive effect is providing dignity and compassion. The higher goal is to be a better friend and, possibly, a better person. At a minimum, your transitions will go smoother and your relationships will improve.

SUMMARY

1. Listening requires your full attention and resisting the urge to respond. The most important part of a conversation can follow after we don't immediately respond.

2. The best conversationalists are those who speak less. Silence is an ally to a good listener.

3. "Tell me more" are the three words everyone wants to hear.

Next Chapter

1. The next chapter deals with transitioning control of your family's wealth to your adult children. Having wealth eventually presents the challenge of deciding when to share information with adult children, when to involve them in decisions, and when to give them control.

2. Inform your children about the family finances gradually and balance the process with the interests, capabilities, and emotional make-up of all participants.

3. Involve your children and transition some control early to build competence and confidence.

CHAPTER 18

SUCCESSFUL WEALTH TRANSITIONS: INVOLVE—INFORM— ENTRUST

Families who use a thoughtful process can prepare the next generation for their roles as stewards and, in the process, bring the family closer together.

Prepare for Stewardship

Wealthy parents of all eras have struggled with the decision when to let "the kids" know about the family finances. There is no simple answer, but at some point, the next generation needs to know. Experience shows it is better for mom and dad to plan when and how to bring the children into the loop than have them learn about family finances from the internet, or worse, in the midst of a crisis.

Communication Is Key

At the heart of a successful wealth transition is a thoughtful communication plan. Helping the next generation become effective stewards is a process, and one that requires time and commitment from all parties. Understanding the importance of keeping family matters private and setting expectations about the role of financial assets in their future are two factors that need to be addressed.

Stages of Wealth Transitions

1. **Inform.** At what age does one begin to share some of the family's financial picture so that the children get a sense of future responsibilities? How does one prepare heirs for stewardship?
2. **Involve.** When should children be part of the conversation so they can begin to understand the legal, tax, and investment issues as well as the needs and viewpoints of other family stakeholders?
3. **Entrust.** When should responsibilities and control be transferred? In what proportions? To whom? A comprehensive communication and education process takes time. Some families begin early and spread it out over a decade or more. Others start later and accelerate the stages. The right plan will depend on the complexity of the family and the readiness of the next generation.

Each Family Is Unique

1. **Blended families** and challenging spousal relationships require special planning and communication. Being "fair" has many interpretations and rarely means "equal."

2. **Family businesses.** Families who operate businesses face issues such as company management and succession, voting control, budget allocations, bonus implications, equity ownership, distributions, and liquidity. There is too much to cover in this context. Let's just agree it's complicated.

3. **Capable and interested.** Families with children who are not interested, not capable, or not yet responsible enough need to consider fiscal oversight. Importantly, the reasons and rationale should be discussed in advance so the plans don't come as a surprise down the road. In the latter two situations, it can be a tough but necessary conversation.

4. **Avoid sibling no-win situations.** Making one sibling the sole trustee for another is almost always a bad idea. If too much or too little is distributed or if investment results are poor, the siblings' relationship could be endangered.

Guidepost I: Inform

They already know. Children have a good understanding of the family's affluence at an early age. When parents tell them that they will be included in discussions regarding private family matters, they will probably feel good about the vote of confidence. It takes time to learn the vocabulary of financial matters and even longer to learn how to apply the concepts. Spacing the education over several years to prepare them should alleviate anxiety about being expected to learn everything right away.

Prepare for independent living. Particularly in cases of significant family wealth, preparing children for the normal responsibilities of life is especially important. Reinforce that they must first be able to handle their own lives—getting jobs, budgeting, saving, getting married, and having children—before they will be expected to be able to handle the responsibilities of family wealth. Begin as early as the mid-teens. If this process is delayed, some benefits may be missed. If the children think they are going to inherit a large family fortune, they may either slack off or be disappointed at the amount they actually inherit.

Eye Dropper, Teaspoon, Glass

1. **Go slowly.** Some families have children attend meetings where some aspects of the finances are revealed. It can help to have your advisors review legal, tax, or investment issues with all of you. This puts the family members on the same side of the table, learning together, and avoids the teacher–pupil dynamic between the parents and children. If a parent is doing all the talking, it can cause tension in some families.

2. **Formal seminars.** Some families have children attend sponsored programs with other "Next-Gen" attendees. Having a third party as part of the process is almost always a good idea.

Both methods begin the exposure to the family's financial situation and inspire awareness of the need for further education.

Guidepost II: Involve

1. **Time for input.** Once the Next-Gen has been "in the know" for a while and you have confidence about their desire to participate, it is time to encourage input. It is a

good idea to establish at the outset how their input will be received and acted upon. Plan how to convey that their input may not be acted upon, at least right away, in order to avoid disappointment and disengagement. Parents who miss this step risk having young adults who expect to have an equal voice in the family's finances far before mom and dad are ready.

2. **Philanthropy as a proving ground.** Often, families use philanthropy as the "test" vehicle. Empower the Next-Gen to make small grants of funds as well as participate in the investment processes while letting them know that mistakes are inevitable and learning from those mistakes is one of the goals. If the Next-Gen does not embrace the offer, consider having them establish a small donor-advised fund in their own name and gifting money into it. Then, it will be their responsibility to manage the investments and allocate the grants.

Guidepost III: Entrust

1. **Your goal.** You want your children to become ethical, educated, and independent. Once they exhibit these traits, give them full control over some of the family money. This might be a rental property, an investment account, a charitable trust, or a division in the family company. Over time, you can increase control and start shifting ownership.

2. **Your role.** I have been told by many CEOs the best promotion they ever had was when they made themselves chair of the company and named someone else CEO. Grooming a successor in business or for the family fortune requires a process. Preparing children to assume

responsibility takes time. Allowing adult children to assume control knowing they are armed with a decade or two of runway of not having to worry about every decision being right is a wonderful position to be in.

Start Planning Now

However you decide to inform and involve your heirs, it will go more smoothly if you have a plan. Done well, you will strengthen and improve family relationships along the way. Final tip: enlist your advisors across finance, risk, legal, and tax for their input regarding content and approach. They will be the grease on the wheels and make everything go a little smoother.

Summary

1. Start slowly and build competence and confidence. As adult children are repeatedly exposed to information, they will understand the lessons and responsibilities as they grow and mature.

2. Some may be interested, some may be capable, some may be interested but incapable, and some may be capable but uninterested.

3. The gradual process allows everyone time and space to find their preferred role and ensure a smooth transition.

Next Chapter

1. A particularly sensitive topic, and one most want to avoid, is prenuptial agreements. How and when to raise the topic is particularly important.

2. There is an optimal way to do everything, and the next chapter offers a process I have seen work many times.

3. Handled correctly, this can be empowering, and the young couple can feel good about maintaining control of their lives while avoiding resenting the "in-laws."

CHAPTER 19

|||||||||||

HOW TO HAVE THE PRENUPTIAL CONVERSATION

One of my friends was asked by a client to speak with her daughter about investing. The daughter was a successful professional and made a lot of money. My friend knew she was going to introduce the topic of getting a prenuptial agreement to the daughter. The key was to do it in a way so the daughter wouldn't think my friend was only bringing it up because she didn't like the daughter's new romantic interest.

After a few minutes of framing the conversation, my friend mentioned that in the daughter's position as an attorney at a very high-profile law firm, she dealt with sensitive topics and occasionally had to offer difficult choices to people. She said she was going to make a comment and that the daughter should put it in a mental box and set it aside. Once the daughter agreed, she recommended the daughter consider a prenuptial agreement before she became serious with someone. Fortunately, the daughter took it well, and they went on to discuss saving and investing.

Forty years of working with families has taught me one thing about prenup conversations: when, where, and how you approach it matters.

Prenuptials and a Spoonful of Sugar

I am often asked about the dos and don'ts of prenuptial agreements. Not legal advice. Rather, how to avoid hurt feelings between the parent and child and especially bruising the relationships with the spouse-to-be and future in-laws.

This is the human part of financial and estate planning. Families of affluence have dealt with asset protection and wealth transfer since the beginning of time, yet the central issue remains: how do families communicate plans to protect the family's assets?

Discuss Early

Before your children get into a serious relationship, talk about it, if possible. Your children already know your family is wealthy. They know where you live, what vacations you take, the boards on which you serve, and the charitable causes you support. They have Googled the assessed value of your home(s) and, if you are a senior executive or director of a public company, seen your compensation data and share ownership in government filings. They know.

Tell them you want to have a family discussion on an important topic. Convey that you also want to hear their thoughts. Stay at a high level to educate them. The conversation lets them know you trust them, and it prepares them for future conversations with more detail. The age and maturity of the child will determine when and how much financial information you want to share, but anytime from about eighteen years and up is probably old enough for the initial discussion.

WHAT TO SAY

Begin by explaining that your family has been fortunate enough to accumulate assets and that there are plans in place to protect them. The plans are intended to protect the family from any number of things, including spurious lawsuits, tragic accidents, and unexpected events. You do not need to go into depth, just establish that plans exist and, in most cases, have existed for years. An important concept to reinforce is that these are family assets—not assets they earned.

I am reminded of a comedy television show in the 1980s about a family with five kids and two successful working parents. The son asked the father, "Dad, are we rich?" The father looked him straight in the eye and responded, "No, we aren't rich. Your mother and I are rich. You have nothing." It was a very funny scene and emphasized that parents have the ability to shape how their children view money and dispel a sense of entitlement.

Back to the prenup conversation. Reinforce that, regarding the assets the children earn in the future, they will decide how they want to handle those. Should they decide to marry, they and their spouse will live independent lives and support themselves, and any assets they accumulate together will be theirs to spend or save as they choose.

If Greater Detail Is Needed

Tell them the family assets are structured to stay in the family and are protected from a variety of unforeseen events. The news headlines are filled with examples of such events, such as spurious lawsuits, health problems (alcohol, drugs, and depression), or other adversities (auto accidents, business failures, gambling debts, etc.).

You may choose to say that at some time in the future, they will enjoy some modest income benefit from family trusts. It is worth mentioning that their eventual spouse may also come from a family of means and have similar planning in place. If the other family does, your children shouldn't feel targeted or demeaned if they find out their fiancé's or fiancée's family wants a prenup as well.

How Will It Be Received?

Explain to your children that some future spouses will be confident in their financial futures and not sensitive to signing a prenuptial agreement. Others may be more sensitive and feel targeted. Preparing your children early is critical so they know you are not singling out their current boyfriend or girlfriend for exclusion.

When a prenuptial agreement is appropriate or will be required, let your children know that as they get serious in their relationship, at some point, they should raise the topic with their partner. It is critical the future spouse is told before the public announcement of their engagement. It is far easier to deal with any unpleasantries prior to the joy and excitement of planning a wedding.

Talking points for your child to their "about to be betrothed":

1. The plans of my family have been in existence for a long time, well before we met.
2. The plans protect my family's assets and do not affect our lives, how we choose to live, or the assets we accumulate together.
3. Our assets and our lives are our own; we control our destiny and are not controlled by the terms of any trust or a trustee.
4. The agreement liberates us from feeling obligated to my parents for our lifestyle, nor can they criticize our spending decisions.
5. I don't have control over the assets, and even if we object, it won't change things.
6. The assets may provide a modest income but ultimately will be passed down to grandchildren.

FIANCÉ TO FIANCÉE CONVERSATION: WHEN AND WHERE

Encourage your child to set aside time at a place where the two of them can speak privately. Allow plenty of time to have the conversation in case someone runs late. Plan a specific activity to follow the conversation that is fun and both are looking forward to. After the conversation, consider going to a nice dinner at a favorite restaurant as a way to cap the evening on a high note.

Finally, after dinner, don't forget dessert! Remember, a spoonful of sugar helps the medicine go down.

Be prepared to have a conversation with your child and their fiancé/fiancée to explain what is in place. You do not need to get into specifics, but you should reassure both why the plans are in place. Offer to speak to the fiancé/fiancée's parents. Same message, same purpose.

Critical to Get Right

Eventually, your child's fiancé or fiancée will need to retain their own lawyer to work through the documents, so if it comes up, be reassured that this is the normal course of things. You cannot pay the costs in any way, and don't let your child pay for it on the side. This must be understood. Sadly, claims of duress and coercion in signing prenups are legendary and have led to agreements being entirely disqualified. The good news for all is that there are assets that require consideration.

Who Should Draft the Agreement?

A lawyer, of course, but who and what type of lawyer? First, it cannot be the same attorney for both parties, as stressed earlier. Some suggest a family/matrimonial/divorce lawyer to "best protect" your interests. However, aggressive posturing by one attorney to get the "best protection" can be upsetting and could be ultimately counterproductive. Many suggest using trust and estate lawyers because they know the ins and outs and are accustomed to collaborating to arrive at agreements. It is an important consideration, so choose wisely.

Don't Delay

It is ideal if both sides agree that the prenuptial agreements will be signed before engagement announcements go out and no later than the wedding date. Set a date, and do not let the date slip. If the lawyers are allowed to wrestle over wording, some will. If the agreement is not signed and the announcements have been mailed, it puts pressure on everyone. No one wants or needs that. The last thing you want going into the final month of planning your child's wedding is to continue to negotiate a contract that could upset the timing of the marriage.

"I don't mean to rush you but the organist has another gig in two hours and the pastor has a tee time at 1:15."

SUMMARY

1. Prenups are common among wealthy families, so don't be surprised if your child's fiancé's or fiancée's family insists on one too. Put it in a positive light—prenups can be viewed as a way to avoid feeling controlled by the in-laws' wealth.

2. Setting the stage for the conversation can make all the difference.

3. Having the conversation early and complete before the engagement announcements go out reduces anxiety.

NEXT CHAPTER

1. The next chapter tackles the difficult topic of transitioning control from elderly parents to adult children. Transitioning control is one of the hardest things about aging. This applies to both the aging parent and the adult children.

2. Whether ceding control over the car keys or the bank account, ensuring dignity and avoiding resentment are paramount.

3. Let the aging person set the terms and the transition well before it becomes necessary.

CHAPTER 20

WHEN IT'S TIME TO TURN OVER THE KEYS

"License and Registration"

It was not a question. It was the second time in a week my eighty-three-year-old grandmother had been asked for them. Even worse, it was the same police officer standing at her car window, staring down at her.

This time, my grandmother had backed into another car in the grocery store parking lot. It must have been the favorite grocery store for many senior citizens because lately there always seemed to be a police cruiser waiting nearby to referee these incidents.

Sensing this might be a pattern and seeing my four-foot-eleven grandmother's difficulty at seeing over the steering wheel, the officer issued her a summons to appear before a judge to determine if she could keep her driver's license. Fortunately for the shareholders of insurance companies worldwide, and to the dismay of the local auto-body industry, the judge said, "No can do."

Although my dad didn't have to be the one leading the conversation about taking away grandmother's driver's license, he did have to deal with the fallout. For many older drivers, their car is their lifeline. Losing the ability to drive can feel like an amputation. Before discussing the car keys, let's talk about transferring control of the family finances.

"Hello again, Mrs. Briody. I see you fixed your left bumper from last week. About your right bumper today, license and registration, please."

Bank and Investment Accounts

I have found financial conversations to be easier and occur earlier than car conversations, but that is not always the case. With the amount of financial scams and elder abuse today, as long as there is trust, most parents are more than willing to involve another person in managing the day to day, paying the bills, and avoiding getting taken advantage of. Unlike driving, where up to 80 percent of drivers feel they are "above average,"[85] when it comes to investing, most people are more self aware.

The lack of personal service by banks, the call centers, the eight-hundred-number toll-free helplines, the chat boxes, the voice menus, and the barrage of emails all encourage parents to involve their children in their finances. From the adult child's perspective, no one wants to find out a parent has been scammed, lost all their savings, or now has to work through years of paperwork to prove they didn't open up ten credit cards or refinance a home.

An easy way to start is to ask to be included in conversations with financial advisors. Get copied on statements and emails. Your parents will still have control but over time will likely take your advice more and more. Occasionally, an aging parent can get too conservative and have large sums sitting in non-interest-bearing accounts, but that is usually the exception. The real risk is if they get talked into buying illiquid investments with large commissions.

---

85   Iain A. McCormick et al., "Comparative Perceptions of Driver Ability—A Confirmation and Expansion," *Accident Analysis and Prevention* 18, no. 3 (June 1986): 205–208, https://doi.org/10.1016/0001-4575(86)90004-7.

For the rest of this section, I will focus on the car keys, but the issues of transferring control from aging parents to adult children are similar and require thoughtful planning and a light touch.

Introducing the Topic

For your mom or dad, the answer to when to give up the keys might be never. However, as vision and motor skills diminish, there may be a time when the topic of planning ahead between an aging parent and their adult child provides an opening.

The next time you have a conversation about estate planning, charitable giving, or tax planning, consider introducing the topic for a future conversation. Empowering your parents to decide under what conditions they would relinquish their keys could pave the way for a conversation that doesn't blow up.

Many people have difficulty driving at night. If this is the case for your parent, the next time there is an evening family get together, consider sending an Uber to pick mom or dad up. Call it a perk and befitting of their stature in life. Make it fun. After dinner, drive your parents home personally. This reinforces your relationship and desire to spend time together. Making familiar the eventual solution of using a driving service should help everyone involved.

Gradual Transitions Help

Handing over the keys is also a metaphor for relinquishing control. All of us need a plan to hand over the financial keys at some point to a trusted person. People are living longer, and as our silver seniors age, they will probably need more help for longer periods of time.

Some people will never want to have the conversation, but it is better to introduce the topic several years prior to it being needed. Look for a story that happened to someone else to introduce the topic and then ask the parent how they would like to have that situation handled if it happens to them. The first step might be to suggest hiring a bill-paying service.

Before *the* Conversation

Whether the topic is money or mobility, if you can, ask vital questions well in advance. "Mom, how does one know when it is time to stop driving?" Or, "How does one know when to involve others in financial management?" Earlier, I mentioned the concept of giving yourself a promotion from CEO to chair of the board. This is essentially the same. Aging parents can have others handle their day-to-day affairs. Consider authorizing the CPA, investment person, and bill-paying service to do so. Consider an unofficial "board of advisors," comprising one or several people, to advise and oversee your parents' affairs.

No one wants to be told what to do. Work toward establishing agreement on reasons why it would make sense to empower others to do more. Personal and financial safety may not be enough of a reason, but the idea of protecting a grandchild's financial future is usually a strong motivation. As for driving, parking lot dents can be ignored, but hitting a mother with a stroller could be the visual image it takes to drive home the point.

Be slow to present a pre-packaged solution to a potential problem that may be far in the future. Today, using a driver service is fun and doesn't carry a stigma or loss of status. Hiring a bill-paying service frees up time and is a sign that one can afford it.

Day of the Conversation

It may be wise to enlist several family members to be part of this conversation. Avoiding being the messenger that gets shot is a good reason, but showing support is the better reason. Also, having a larger group helps.

Should you involve an outsider? If you are fortunate enough to have a family friend who your parents respect and trust, they may be helpful. To have the best possible chance of a smooth transition, the timing and reason for the conversation should be known, if not obvious. A car accident, a health problem, or something mom or dad recently said or did are good transition points.

If this is the first time the subject has been raised, it may be a very tough conversation. If it is one of a series of compassionate discussions and the alternatives to keep mom and dad active and involved are known and familiar, you will have a much better chance at reducing dented fenders and keeping the peace at home.

There are no magic bullets, but thoughtful, advanced planning combined with love, compassion, and acceptable alternatives will go a long way toward keeping people safe and maintaining family harmony.

SUMMARY

1. Achieving peace of mind is enabled by achieving financial independence. Financial independence means not worrying about the day to day. Freeing aging parents from the tedium of bill paying and the safety concerns of driving can be liberating.

2. Prep your parents for the conversation well before it needs to occur. Promote your parents, hire a driver, and have someone else worry about the details.

3. Change is hard, especially as we get older. Have parents set the terms and timing of the gradual transitions.

CONCLUDING
THOUGHTS

The goal of this book is to provide simple steps for the reader to understand there is more to managing wealth than just managing money.

*The main point is **money is not the main point.***

There are steps that should be taken and processes that should be followed to make the most of the family and financial gifts we have. Administered well, assets that have been accumulated and lessons that have been passed along can reduce stress about one's financial future and enable us and our families to focus on living fulfilled lives.

What we do with our lives and our resources, how we interact with our family and community, and the lasting impact we have on the lives of others are what make us rich. Having assets can provide security and stability but should never be the objective. Accompanying the stewardship of wealth is the responsibility to ensure it helps your family and, if you have extra, your community and society.

Peace of mind is the objective. Financial independence is an important part but just a stop on the road to peace of mind. Helping others get there is my vocation and avocation. I hope you have enjoyed what you learned and, in time, it will enable you to help others learn even more.

"Spend each day trying to be a little wiser than you were when you woke up."
-Charlie Munger-

ACKNOWLEDGMENTS

First, of course, I must thank my family—my wife, Dee, and my daughters, Alexie, Catherine, and Hollis. For years, when I worked long hours and commuted to different cities pursuing "the dream," they were my biggest fans and supporters. To my parents, who raised six children under financial challenges and taught us the invaluable lessons that all good parents teach. To my siblings who, when my self-esteem ballooned to irrational propositions, kept me in check.

I want to thank those who have taught me about values, honor, and integrity: the Sisters of the Holy Cross, the Lasallian Christian Brothers, and the Augustinians at Villanova. In later years, the Society of the Sacred Heart and the Order of Malta have had an outsized influence on my development, for which I am deeply grateful. I am still a work in progress.

Two of the people whose leadership has had the greatest influence on me are my former bosses and lifelong friends Tom Matthews and Wayne Hutton. They had the unique ability to run very successful businesses and teach by example while still being regarded as close friends by thousands of people who worked for them.

I want to thank a few professional friends, especially those from Smith Barney and the Association of Professional Investment Consultants, with whom I spent so much time—Mark Curtis, Sandee Smith, Lori Van Dusen, and Jim Stoker.

The original team at Citigroup Smith Barney's Private Wealth Management, who helped to create the industry's leading ultra-high-net-worth platform, are responsible for so much of the acclaim the firm enjoyed—Chris di Bonaventura, Rosalie Berman, Judy Spalthoff, Janine Miller Lyons, Christy Mayo Hahn, Lauren Male Crandall, Jocelyn Warner Lowrey, Sam Anderson, Erin Olpher Houston, Neil Sumter, Ted Noll, John Sullivan, Lisa McGreevy Ryan, Shirl Penney, and Peter White from Citi Private Bank all enabled it to become a force.

Rebekah Teesdale, Cathy Tran, Rachel Johnson Noonan, and Jim Chandler were partners here in Washington, DC, and, with Michael Hickey, all helped develop the tools we use today.

My good friend and mentor Harold Zirkin is one of the best portfolio managers I have met. Bryson Cook, who dispenses tax, trust, and business advice to owners of large, complex, private businesses. Both should be in the Pantheon of their respective fields.

Almost twenty years ago, Joe Tranfo encouraged me to write this book and John Groom, a friend of forty years and independent publisher, showed me how to do it.

I want to thank my publishing team at Scribe, particularly Eric Jorgenson and Chip Blake, both of whom were instrumental in getting this across the finish line. Chip took a very weak first draft and molded it into this final product. I never minded making the suggested edits but was embarrassed about how much Chip had to do. Thanks, pal.

My business partner and friend Eliza Jeffereis, who tirelessly kept me organized and the momentum going, as well as my partner at Promethium Advisors, Ed Giese.

The final word of thanks has to go to our clients, many of whom have written kind words about our relationship, who have entrusted me with their families' financial futures. Without them, there would be no book.

ABOUT THE AUTHOR

CHRISTOPHER F. POCH, FOUNDER AND CEO OF PROMETHIUM ADVISORS, LLC

Some financial advisors had mentors who were family members in the business. Others had mentors who provided examples of hard work, customer service, and faith in the free-enterprise system.

For Christopher Poch, it was the latter. His interest in the markets and all things financial was gleaned from his father, a small businessman who unknowingly set in motion what would become Chris's career in wealth management.

From the time he was eight years old, Chris held jobs ranging from bagging nails to loading cars to selling door to door. He learned that serving the customer well is central to success. While still in college and holding down two part-time jobs, he passed the examination to sell life insurance. Just out of college, he worked for Merrill Lynch and then joined E. F. Hutton as an account executive.

By 2001, Chris had moved to New York, had founded Private Wealth Management at Citigroup Smith Barney, and carried the title of Managing Director. Under his leadership, his unit was recognized by leading publications as the global leader in advising ultra-high-net-worth families.

In 2010, Chris returned to his hometown of Washington, DC, to run the mid-Atlantic region for Bessemer Trust. In 2016, he wrote his first book, *Managing Your Wealth: A Must-Read for Affluent Families*, and in 2017, he resumed managing private portfolios and publishing wealth-management and market commentary.

Even after growing his business to more than $1 billion in assets under management, Chris felt limited in his ability to recommend investment solutions he felt his clients really needed.

So, in 2024, Chris forged his own path, launching the independent firm Promethium Advisors, LLC. Based in Bethesda, Maryland, Chris's firm serves family offices and high-net-worth individuals and is designed "for the next generation of advice," serving clients as true fiduciaries.

In *Money and Meaning*, Chris relates a journey spanning more than four decades that imbued him with a level of experience few can offer, including:

- Life in the big brokerages like Smith Barney—and what changes he saw at the firm and in the industry at-large in the time leading up to the 2008 financial crisis.
- Why he passed on multiple lucrative offers from brokerage and private equity firms to open a firm answering solely to clients.

- How having his own firm allowed him to create a business that aligned with his vision and values.
- Choosing to "shrink to grow," meaning leaving certain relationships behind—and how it provided a clearer path to long-term satisfaction and profitability.

Chris is an industry visionary with accolades that include founding the industry-leading UHNW Platform, serving as Vice Chair of The Private Bank and the Global Head of Citibank's International Private Bank, and being the past president of the Association of Professional Investment Consultants and second recipient of its lifetime achievement award.

Chris provides a rare insider's view from a managing director of a global Wall Street powerhouse as well as the observations of an objective outsider offering a critical assessment of the investment industry's shortcomings. There's much to learn from his story, with key takeaways for clients, advisors, and business owners alike.

In memory of my parents, Robert A. Poch and Janice L. Poch

Poch Hardware ©1989 Potomac, Maryland   5/500 Joan Jusade

Poch Hardware, Potomac Village
Potomac, Maryland
1968–1992

STAY CONNECTED

No matter where you are on your financial journey, insight and connection are essential components of lasting success. Stay connected with the author and continue your path forward with confidence.

PROMETHIUM MARKET COMMENTARY

Receive Forethinking by Promethium, our quarterly commentary identifying market trends and strategic insights.

Scan: QR Code

REQUEST A MEETING

Looking for personalized guidance or a trusted financial partner? Request a one-on-one meeting to talk through your goals and see if we may be able to help.

Scan: QR Code

DISCLAIMER

It must be stated at the outset that, despite best intentions, the opinions and conclusions in this book are drawn from personal experience and will differ from many. Some recommendations do not follow conventional wisdom nor common industry practices. Many points can be argued differently and perhaps not incorrectly. I am aware that I will not always be right and that, in the eyes of peers, some of my views may not be popular.

I do not claim to have the ability to forecast markets nor be right on everything. The advice rendered in this book must always be taken in the context of having "more money" is not the goal. Doing the "best" or always being "right" is also not the end game. Instead, this book encourages the reader to seek peace of mind, which requires a level of financial independence, resulting in happiness. Perhaps my financial bar is set lower than others to achieve what I consider a higher bar. Those priorities will be for you, the reader, to judge for yourself.

Advisory Services offered through Promethium, a registered investment advisor with the US Securities and Exchange Commission. This material is intended for informational purposes only. It should not be construed as legal or tax advice and is not intended to replace the advice of a qualified attorney or tax advisor. The information contained in this presentation has been compiled from third-party sources and is believed to be reliable as of the date of this report. Past performance is not indicative of future returns and diversification neither assures a profit nor guarantees against loss in a declining market. Investments involve risk and are not guaranteed.

The information being provided is strictly as a courtesy. When you link to any of these websites provided here, the Firm makes no representation as to the completeness or accuracy of information provided at these sites. Nor is the company liable for any direct or indirect technical or system issues or any consequences arising out of your access to or your use of third-party technologies, sites, information, and programs made available through. When you access one of these sites, you assume total responsibility and risk for your use of the sites you are linking to.

This material should not be construed as legal or tax advice and is not intended to replace the advice of a qualified attorney or tax advisor. The information contained in this presentation has been compiled from third-party sources and is believed to be reliable. All opinions and views constitute our judgments as of the date of writing and are subject to change at any time without notice. This presentation is not an offer or solicitation to buy or sell securities and may not be construed as investment advice and does not give investment recommendations.

Diversification neither assures a profit nor guarantees against loss in a declining market.

Different types of investments involve varying degrees of risk, and there can be no assurance that any specific investment will either be suitable or profitable for a client or prospective client's investment portfolio. Historical performance results for investment indices and/or categories generally do not reflect the deduction of transaction and/or custodial charges, the deductions of an investment management fee, nor the impact of taxes, the incurrence of which would have the effect of decreasing historical performance results.

In regard to this testimonial and/or endorsement for Promethium; (i) the individuals providing the testimonial and/or endorsement may be current clients; (ii) the individuals have not been compensated; and (iii) this does not pose any material conflicts of interest on the part of the person giving the testimonial and/or endorsement resulting from the adviser's relationship with such person.